"Paul Tripp constantly turns us back to the life-giving power of the gospel and God's unfailing grace. Parenting our children is one of life's greatest challenges, and Paul points us to the one thing that can make a difference—a genuine encounter with the living God."

TobyMac, hip-hop recording artist; music producer; songwriter

"Simply put, I read everything that Paul Tripp writes. I can't afford to miss one word."

Ann Voskamp, *New York Times* best-selling author, *One Thousand Gifts*

"This is the most meaningful book I have read all year. It is both theological and practical, a rare combination for a parenting book. For years, people have asked me to write a book on parenting. After reading this, I am convinced that I could never write one better than this. I'm so glad I read this, but I wish I could have read it twenty years ago. After reading *Parenting*, I was torn. Part of me wanted to sit, cry, and confess all of my failures as a parent. The other part wanted to scream with excitement for the tremendous insight I now have to be a better parent."

Francis Chan, *New York Times* best-selling author, *Crazy Love* and *Forgotten God*

"I cannot recommend this book highly enough. It is simply outstanding. This is Tripp at his best: he shows us the big picture of life with Christ and gets down to the nitty-gritty specifics of walking by grace through faith. Tripp's manifesto is about more than simply our duty as parents—it's about our privilege of being ambassadors of Jesus Christ to our kids. Moms and dads from every culture will benefit from Tripp's call for us to live in light of the grace and hope we have in Jesus."

Gloria Furman, pastor's wife, Redeemer Church of Dubai; author, *The Pastor's Wife* and *Missional Motherhood*

"This book is so timely for me. My bride and I are raising four children aged five and under, and we need help! It's easy to find books with parenting tips on how to correct our children's behavior, but Paul Tripp's book goes far beyond behavior; he takes the reader to the source of the problem—the heart. If we understand our children at a heart level and have a proper understanding of the gospel, then we can parent them as God intends. Paul Tripp has written a simple yet profound book. Parents, you need to read this now. You will surely be blessed."

Webb Simpson, professional golfer; 2012 U.S. Open Champion

"I am an imperfect parent. You probably are too. Buy this book and soak in it. This is not another '5 Steps to Becoming a Perfect Parent'—instead, Tripp wants us to see our relationship to God and to our children through a big-picture lens. My wife and I are always-go-never-stop parents of young children. If you know the feeling, this book will be both challenging and refreshing, and ultimately it will be a great blessing to your journey. Tripp has made me think in a fresh way about the extremely important and tremendously challenging task that is everyday parenting. To raise up a child is a great responsibility—let us take it up with reverence, joy, and a loving heart!"

Jacob Tamme, former NFL® tight end

Parenting

Crossway Books by Paul David Tripp

40 Days of Faith

40 Days of Grace

40 Days of Hope

40 Days of Love

A Quest for More: Living for Something Bigger Than You

A Shelter in the Time of Storm: Meditations on God and Trouble

Age of Opportunity: A Biblical Guide for Parenting Teens

Awe: Why It Matters for Everything We Think, Say, and Do

Broken-Down House: Living Productively in a World Gone Bad

Come, Let Us Adore Him: A Daily Advent Devotional

Dangerous Calling: Confronting the Unique Challenges of Pastoral Ministry

Do You Believe: 12 Historic Doctrines to Change Your Everyday Life

Forever: Why You Can't Live without It

How People Change (with Timothy S. Lane)

Instruments in the Redeemer's Hands: People in Need of Change Helping People in Need of Change

Journey to the Cross: A 40-Day Lenten Devotional

Lead: 12 Gospel Principles for Leadership in the Church

Lost in the Middle: Midlife and the Grace of God

Marriage: 6 Gospel Commitments Every Couple Needs to Make

My Heart Cries Out: Gospel Meditations for Everyday Life

New Morning Mercies: A Daily Gospel Devotional

New Morning Mercies for Teens: A Daily Gospel Devotional

Parenting: 14 Gospel Principles That Can Radically Change Your Family

Reactivity: How the Gospel Transforms Our Actions and Reactions

Redeeming Money: How God Reveals and Reorients Our Hearts

Relationships: A Mess Worth Making (with Timothy S. Lane)

Sex in a Broken World: How Christ Redeems What Sin Distorts

Suffering: Gospel Hope When Life Doesn't Make Sense

Sunday Matters: 52 Devotionals to Prepare Your Heart for Church

War of Words: Getting to the Heart of Your Communication Struggles

Whiter Than Snow: Meditations on Sin and Mercy

PARENTING

*14 Gospel Principles That Can
Radically Change Your Family*

PAUL DAVID TRIPP

CROSSWAY®

WHEATON, ILLINOIS

Parenting: 14 Gospel Principles That Can Radically Change Your Family

© 2016, 2024 by Paul David Tripp

Published by Crossway
        1300 Crescent Street
        Wheaton, Illinois 60187

Cover design: Josh Dennis

Cover image: Exopixel, Shutterstock.com / Prapass, Shutterstock.com
        Roman Tsubin, Shutterstock.com

First printing 2016

Reprinted with study questions 2024

Printed in the United States of America

Hardcover ISBN: 978-1-4335-9360-4
ePub ISBN: 978-1-4335-9362-8
PDF ISBN: 978-1-4335-9361-1

Library of Congress Cataloging-in-Publication Data
Names: Tripp, Paul David, 1950– author.
Title: Parenting : 14 gospel principles that can radically change your family / Paul David Tripp.
Description: Wheaton : Crossway, 2016. | Includes index.
Identifiers: LCCN 2016011594 (print) | LCCN 2016025563 (ebook) | ISBN 9781433551932 (hc) | ISBN 9781433551963 (epub) | ISBN 9781433551949 (pdf) | ISBN 9781433551956 (mobi)
Subjects: LCSH: Parents—Religious life. | Parenting—Religious aspects—Christianity. | Child rearing—Religious aspects—Christianity.
Classification: LCC BV4529 .T755 2016 (print) | LCC BV4529 (ebook) | DDC 248.8/45—dc23 LC record available at https://lccn.loc.gov/2016011594

Crossway is a publishing ministry of Good News Publishers.

LB		34	33	32	31	30	29	28	27	26	25	24
13	12	11	10	9	8	7	6	5	4	3	2	1

To the team of people who partner with me
to do what God has called me to do.

Because you love God,
are dedicated to your calling,
and are smarter than me,
I am blessed every day by your work
and freed to do mine.

Contents

Introduction

Ambassadors

YOUR HOUSE IS NOISY and not as clean as you'd like it to be, you and your husband haven't been out together for a long time, the laundry has piled up once again, you just discovered there's nothing to pack for lunch, you've just broken up another fight, the schedule for the week looks impossible, you seem to have more expenses than money, none of the people around seem to be satisfied, and you feel exhausted and unappreciated.

In the middle of all the endless parenting activities, many parents get lost. They are doing lots of things, lots of good things, but they don't know why. They've been swallowed up into the daily grind of parenting, but they've lost sight of what it is that they're working for or building toward. They don't understand why these ones that they love have the power to pull such irritation and frustration out of them. The menial tasks that they have to do day after day get reduced to an endless catalog of unattractive duties that don't seem to have any overarching vision that holds them all together and sanctifies them with meaning and purpose.

As I've traveled the world talking about parenting, I've had thousands of exhausted parents ask me for more effective strategies for this or that, when what they really need is a *big picture parenting worldview* that can explain, guide, and motivate all the things that God calls them to do as parents. If you are going not only to cope, but to thrive with vision and joy as a parent, you need more than the next book that gives you seven steps to solving whatever. You need God's helicopter view of what he's called you to do. You need a *big gospel parenting worldview* that will not only make sense of your task, but will change the way you approach it.

Yes, you did read it right. I am deeply persuaded that what is missing in most Christian parent's parenting are the big grand perspectives and principles of the gospel of Jesus Christ. These perspectives and principles are radical and counterintuitive. They're simply not natural for us, but they're essential to being what you're supposed to be and doing what you're supposed to do as a parent. When you parent with what the gospel says about God, you, your world, your children, and God's grace, you not only approach parenting in brand-new ways, but you carry the burden of parenting in a very different way.

I have to be honest here. I wrote a parenting book (*Age of Opportunity*), and I told myself and repeatedly told others that I was not about to write another one, yet here I am doing just that. Why? Because as I listened to people tell me how they had used *Age* in the lives of their teenagers, I became increasingly uncomfortable. I kept thinking, "No, that's not exactly it," or "No, that's not what I meant," or "No, there's something missing." It took a while, but it finally hit me that what bothered me in these conversations and what was missing in these parents was the gospel that was the foundation behind everything that I wrote. So with the publisher's encouragement, I decided to write a parenting book, but not the typical kind. This will not be a book of practical strategies for dealing with children at the various ages of their development. This book will not provide practical steps for dealing with the kinds of things every parent faces. This book is meant to be a reorienting book. It is meant to give you a new way of thinking about and responding to everything that will be on your plate as a parent. This book is meant to give you vision, motivation, renewed strength, and the rest of heart that every parent needs. It is written to give you the *big gospel picture* of the task to which your Savior has called you.

Lost in the Middle of Your Own Parenting Story

The big picture starts with knowing who you are as a parent. I don't mean your name, address, and Social Security number. I mean who you are in relation to who God is, to what life is about, and to who your children are. If you don't have this "who you are" perspective right, you will miss the essence of what God has called you to, and you will do things that no parent should do.

I am afraid that parenting confusion and dysfunction often begin with parents having an *ownership* view of parenting. It is seldom expressed and often unconscious, but it operates on this perspective of parenting: *"These children belong to me, so I can parent them in the way I see fit."* Now, no parent actually says that, but it tends to be the perspective that most of us fall into. In the press of overwhelming responsibilities and a frenetic schedule, we lose sight of what parenting is really about. We look at our children as belonging to us, and we end up doing things that are short-sighted, not helpful in the long-run, more reactive than goal-oriented, and outside of God's great, big, wise plan.

Ownership parenting is not overtly selfish, abusive, or destructive; it involves a subtle shift in thinking and motivation that puts us on a trajectory that leads our parenting far away from God's design. This shift is subtle because it takes place in little, mundane moments of family life—moments that seem so small and insignificant that the people in the middle of them are unaware of the movement that has taken place. But the shifts are significant precisely because they do take place in insignificant little moments, because those little moments are the addresses where our parenting lives. Very little of our parenting takes place in grand significant moments that have stopped us in our tracks and commanded our full attention; parenting takes place on the fly when we're not really paying attention and are greeted with things that we did not know we were going to be dealing with that day. It's the repeated cycle of little unplanned moments that is the soul-shaping workroom of parenting.

Ownership parenting is motivated and shaped by what parents want *for* their children and *from* their children. It is driven by a vision of what we want our children to be and what we want our children to give us in return. (I'll say more about this later). It seems right, it feels right, and it does many good things, but it is foundationally misguided and misdirected and will not produce what God intends in the lives that he has entrusted to our care. There, I've said it! Good parenting, which does what God intends it to do, begins with this radical and humbling recognition that our children don't actually belong to us. Rather, every child in every home, everywhere on the globe, belongs to the One who created him or her. Children are God's possession (see Ps. 127:3) for his purpose. That means that his plan for parents is that we would be his agents in the lives of these ones that have been formed into his image and entrusted to our care.

The word that the Bible uses for this intermediary position is *ambassador*. It really is the perfect word for what God has called parents to be and to do. The only thing an ambassador does, if he's interested in keeping his job, is to faithfully represent the message, methods, and character of the leader who has sent him. He is not free to think, speak, or act independently. Everything he does, every decision he makes, and every interaction he has must be shaped by this one question: "What is the will and plan of the one who sent me?" The ambassador does not represent his own interest, his own perspective, or his own power. He does everything as an ambassador, or he has forgotten who he is and he will not be in his position for long.

Parenting is *ambassadorial* work from beginning to end. It is not to be shaped and directed by personal interest, personal need, or cultural perspectives. Every parent everywhere is called to recognize that they have been put on earth at a particular time and in a particular location to do one thing in the lives of their children. What is that one thing? It is God's will. Here's what this means at street level: parenting is not first about what we want *for* our children or *from* our children, but about what God in grace has planned to do through us *in* our children. To lose sight of this is to end up with a relationship with our children that at the foundational level is neither Christian nor true parenting because it has become more about our will and our way than about the will and way of our Sovereign Savior King.

I want to say right here and now that I am very bad at what I am now writing about. I like sovereignty, I like ownership, and I like having my will done on earth as God's will is done in heaven! I often treated my four children (who are now grown) as if they were my possessions. I often suffered from ambassadorial schizophrenia—at moments losing my mind, taking my parenting into my own hands, and doing things that I shouldn't have done. I was often a very poor example of joyful submission to God's law. I was often a very poor representative of God's grace. I was often more propelled by fear than I was by faith. I often wanted short-term gain more than I wanted long-term transformation. There were moments when I forgot who I was, lost my mind, and did things that really didn't make any sense, or at least weren't very helpful.

I am going to ask you right now to be honest and admit that you're like me. You too lose your way and forget who you are in the middle of the endless, repetitive tasks of parenting the children entrusted to your care. There are moments when you too lose your mind. There are times when what you're saying and doing just isn't helpful and definitely not ambassadorial.

You just sat down fifteen minutes ago after giving your five-times-a-day lecture on loving your neighbor and are feeling momentarily good about how it went; now you're back in the family room with your iPad. Before you have a chance to hit the button for your favorite magazine app, you hear angry voices floating down the hallway from the very room you were just in. You can't believe it! You're tired, and it feels personal. You want to throw your iPad through the window, but you know doing so would break both. You wish the insanity would stop so you could enjoy just one sane personal moment. You don't regret that you have children, but at this point you kinda wish they weren't *your* children. You're angry, and you're about to lose your mind, forgetting who you are and what you've been called to do. Emotion is propelling you down the hallway, and that emotion is not love. An agenda is motivating you, and that agenda is not grace. You are in the room and yelling before you even realize you have left your family room chair. You're talking, but you're not thinking. You're reacting, but what you're doing is not parenting. You're meting out a catalog of punishments, which you're later going to have to enforce. You threaten worse if you have to come down that hallway again. You leave the room mumbling something about how you would have never thought of acting that way when you were their age. You throw yourself into the chair, grab your iPad, and open the app, but you're not paying attention because your emotions are raging. "What do I have to do to get them to listen, to get them to obey for once?" you ask yourself as your emotions calm. You feel a bit guilty, and because you do, you try to convince yourself that your kids deserved it.

Who of us hasn't been there? What parent can look back on the days, weeks, months, and years that he had with his children with no regret whatsoever? It is so important to humbly recognize how counterintuitive *ambassadorial* parenting is and to seek the rescue and the power to remember that only God in his amazing grace can provide. Sin makes us all more natural owners than ambassadors. Sin makes us all more demanding than patient. Sin causes all of us to find punishment more natural than grace. Sin makes all of us more able to see and be distressed by the sin, weakness, and failure of others than we are about our own. Sin makes it easier for us to talk *at* other people rather than listening *to* them. Here's what all of this means: the thing that constantly gets in the way of our ambassadorial calling as parents is us! Humbly confessing this is the first step in your ambassadorship.

Owner or Ambassador?

Perhaps you're thinking at this point, "Paul, I don't think I treat my children like they're my possessions. I think I try to serve God in the lives of my children, but I'm not sure." Well, I want to help you. Maybe the place to begin is to observe that few parents conduct themselves like total owners or complete ambassadors. I think for most of us *ownership parenting* and *ambassadorial parenting* represent a daily battle that is fought on the turf of our hearts. We are constantly torn between what we want and what God wants. We are constantly pulled one way by what we think is best and the other way by what God says is best. We at one moment are way too influenced by the values of the surrounding culture and at another moment are very serious in our conviction that a biblical way of thinking must shape our parenting. Sometimes we just want our children to behave so our lives could be easier, while at other moments we accept the fact that parenting is spiritual warfare.

It is helpful to think through, at a practical level, the difference between ownership and ambassadorial parenting. I therefore distinguish between these two models of parenting in four areas that every parent somehow, in some way, deals with: identity, work, success, and reputation. The way you think about and interact with these four things will expose and define who you think you are as a parent and what you think your job is in raising your children.

1. Identity: Where you look to find your sense of who you are.

Owner: Owner parents tend to look to get their identity, meaning, purpose, and inner sense of well-being from their children. Their children tend to be saddled with the unbearable burden of their parents' sense of self-worth. I have to say this: parenting is a miserable place to look for your identity, if for no other reason than the fact that every parent parents sinners. Children come into the world with significant brokenness inside of them that causes them to push against the authority, wisdom, and guidance of their parents. Parents who are looking to their children for identity tend to take their children's failures personally, as if they were done against them intentionally, and respond to their children with personal hurt and anger. But the reality is that God simply does not give you children in order for you to feel that your life is worthwhile.

Ambassador: Parents who approach parenting as representatives come to it with a deep sense of identity and are motivated by meaning and purpose. They don't need to get that from their children because they have gotten it from the One whom they represent: the Lord Jesus Christ. Because of this they are freed from coming to their children hoping that they will get from them what no child is able to give. They are freed from asking family life to give them life because they have found life and their hearts are at rest. Because of this, they are now freed to forget themselves and parent with the selflessness and sacrifice that ambassadorial parenting requires.

2. Work: What you define as the work you have been called to do.

Owner: Owner parents think that their job is to turn their children into something. They have a vision of what they want their children to be, and they think that their work as parents is to use their authority, time, money, and energy to form their children into what they have conceived that they should be. I have counseled many children who were breaking under the burden of the constant pressure of parents who had a concrete vision and were determined that these children would be what these parents had decided they would be. Owner parents tend to think that they have the power and personal resources to mold their children into the children they envision.

Ambassador: Parents who really do understand that they are never anything more than representatives of someone greater, wiser, more powerful, and more gracious than they are know that their daily work is not to turn their children into anything. They have come to understand that they have no power whatsoever to change their children and that without God's wisdom they wouldn't even know what is best for their children. They know that what they have been called to be are instruments in the hands of One who is gloriously wise and is the giver of the grace that has the power to rescue and transform the children who have been entrusted to their care. They are not motivated by a vision of what they want their children to be, but by the potential of what grace could cause their children to be.

3. Success: What you define success to be.

Owner: These parents tend to be working toward a specific catalog of indicators in the lives of their children that would tell them that they have been successful parents. Things like academic performance, athletic achievement, musical ability, and social likability become the horizontal markers of how well they have done their jobs. Now these things are not unimportant, but they simply are unable to measure successful parenting. Good parents don't always produce good kids, and parents should constantly be asking themselves where they get the set of values that tell them whether they have "good" kids or not. I am afraid that many good parents live with long-term feelings of failure because their children have not turned out the way they hoped.

Ambassador: These parents have faced the scary truth that they have no power at all to produce anything in their children. Because of this they haven't attached their definition of successful parenting to a catalog of horizontal outcomes. Successful parenting is not first about what you've produced; rather, it's first about what you have done. Let me say it this way: successful parenting is not about achieving goals (that you have no power to produce) but about being a usable and faithful tool in the hands of the One who alone is able to produce good things in your children.

4. Reputation: What tells people who you are and what you're about.

Owner: Owner parents unwittingly turn their children into their trophies. They tend to want to be able to parade their children in public to the applause of the people around them. This is why so many parents struggle with the crazy, zany phases that their children go through as they are growing up. They're not so much concerned about what that craziness says about their children, but what it says about *them*. Children in these homes feel both the burden of carrying their parents' reputation and the sting of their disappointment and embarrassment. Owner parents tend to be angry and disappointed with their children, not first because they've broken God's law, but because whatever they have done has brought hassle and embarrassment to them.

Ambassador: These parents have come to understand that parenting sinners will expose them to public misunderstanding and embarrassment somehow, someway. They have come to accept the humbling messiness of the job God has called them to do. And they understand that if their children grow and mature in life and godliness, they become not so much their trophies, but trophies of the Savior that they have sought to serve. For them, it's God who does the work and God who gets the glory; they are just gratified that they were able to be the tools that God used.

Are you ready to chuck the burden of being an owner and begin to experience what parenting looks like when you know that you have been called to represent the message, methods, and character of *the* Owner of your kids? Are you ready to be freed from the burden of trying to create change, and to experience the rest to be found in functioning as a tool of the One whose grace alone has the power to change? Then this book is for you. It is meant to yank you out of the daily grind and to consider the big picture of what God is inviting you to be part of as he works in the hearts and lives of your children. It is meant to help you see how radically different parenting becomes when you quit trying to produce change and become a willing tool of the grace that rescues, forgives, and changes. Each chapter will introduce and explain a parenting principle that takes that grace seriously. Many of you are exhausted, discouraged, and frustrated. How about considering a new and better way: the way of grace?

1

Calling

Principle: Nothing is more important in your life than being one of God's tools to form a human soul.

YOU'RE FRUSTRATED BECAUSE for some reason on this particular Tuesday night your two-year-old daughter has decided that she will not, under any circumstance, pressure, or threat, eat her peas. You're not asking her to eat poison; they're peas—silly little, round, green vegetal orbs! What in the world is in her mind right now? Why do these little tasks have to be so hard?

You can't believe it—another note from his teacher. This is the fifth note in three weeks, and he's only in kindergarten! For some reason he won't stop talking in class during the moments when he's not supposed to be talking. He talks when the teacher talks. He talks when other students are trying to talk. He talks with his mouth full during lunchtime. He talks his way through his nap time. He talks when you're trying to talk to him about talking too much! And you thought that finally sending him to school would simplify your life.

It's been one of those days. You're convinced it's a sibling conspiracy against you. It feels as if your children have plotted together to make this day particularly difficult. It feels as if it's you against The Legion of Rebellious Ones. You've lost your patience too many times. You've said and done embarrassing things. You raised your voice and made ominous threats, but nothing has seemed to help. You've lost control of your own house and, silently and with a bit of guilt, you wish for the simple days of before.

You've just had one of the best conversations you've ever had as a parent; it's hard to imagine that an eleven-year-old could be so deep, so philosophical. You were caught off guard; you had no idea that in this passing moment time would stop and profound considerations would be on the table. You didn't feel very prepared; you stumbled over your words. You hoped what you said was helpful, understandable, and wise. You hope the way you said things would open up more conversations. You just wish an alarm would have gone off, telling you that things were about to get very serious.

She seems embarrassed by you. It really does hurt. She used to run into your arms for comfort and love. She loved to hold your hand as she skipped her way through the mall. She would dress up in your clothes and pretend to be you. She'd get on a stool in the kitchen and "help" you cook dinner. She would run to you with that great big smile when she won the ribbon at gymnastics. Now she wants you to drop her off at the mall and asks you please not to come in. She doesn't really want you to pick her up from school and when you do, she wants you to park down the street. She doesn't bring many friends home and when she does, they hide in her room out of sight and separate from you. You want her to run up to you and bury her head in your chest and say, "I love you. Mommy," like she used to, but you don't think she will.

You've taken them to a movie; it's the one thing you all enjoy doing as a family. It was billed as a fun family comedy, but it's been filled with sexual innuendo from beginning to end. You didn't catch the last part of the movie because your mind had wandered away thinking of what you should say, how you should handle what your children were exposed to. How much did they understand? If you talk to them, will you just be opening a can of worms? Is it time to have a very frank talk about sex? Are you ready? Are they ready? How will you do it? When will you do it? You wish you had a script to follow.

As you carry the final bit of his stuff up to his dorm room, you tell yourself that he's a good kid, but you really wonder if he's ready. You look at him, and you don't see a university student; you see a leaky-nosed, scuffed-kneed six-year-old begging to spend the night with a friend. He did okay in high school; no drugs, sex, or jail time. He was determined to go away to college, somewhere new, somewhere different from home. You worry that his dorm has double the students that were in his high school. The girls walking around the hallways of his coed dorm make you uncomfortable. You want to grab him, throw him and his pile of stuff into the car, and get out of there as fast as you can before you lose him completely. He tells you not to worry, that he will be okay, but it doesn't help. You pray with him before you leave, but you're still a wreck. You ask him to call later, but you don't think he will.

She finished college. She's come back home while she looks for a job. You thought that your parenting days were over, but they're clearly not. The state of her room, her choice of friends, and the way she spends her time make you wonder if she is ready to be a full-fledged adult. You have mixed emotions. You loved having your house and your time back again, but you missed being a mom. Now she's back and it's different. You know she still needs you, that she'll need guidance as she makes her launch, but you're not sure she realizes it. Every night you try to go to bed and sleep at the normal time, but you never really get to sleep until you hear the door and know she's home safe. You're tired of being a parent and thankful that she's home, all at the same time.

You're haunted by regret. You don't want to be, but you are; not about anything big, but about all those little moments of failure. You remember the little promises you made that you got too busy to keep. The moments when you yelled when you should have been listening. You remember how hard it was to have children and be fair and how often you failed. You remember falling asleep at recitals and hope they never knew. You remember making ridiculous threats and hope they don't remember as well as you do. You remember that time you stopped the van, made them all get out, and told them that you wouldn't let them back in until they could get along with one another. You remember that it was easier to announce the law than to give grace. You'd like to be free of regret, but you're not.

What is everything I just described about? What unifies all these parental scenarios? They are all about a calling—one of the most significant callings that could ever be laid in the lap of a human being. If you would stop and think about its full ramifications, it would make you run away unless it had already made you too weak in the knees. In a way it's insane for anyone to actually think that they could take this on. You'd have to be delusional to think that you're actually prepared. It has the quality of standing before a 747 and telling yourself that you could pick it up if you wanted to. It seems that this could possibly be the one mistake of an otherwise perfect God. Is it really true that God asks parents to be his agents-on-hand for the forming of a human soul? Really? Let's consider the enormity of God's plan and what it means for you as parents.

Parents as Treasure Hunters

Here's what you need to understand: everything you do and say in your life, every choice that you make, and everything you decide to invest in is a reflection of a system of internalized values in your heart. As beings made in God's likeness, we do not function by instinct. Rather, we are value-motivated human beings. Your words, your time commitments, your finances, your emotional highs and lows, your relationships, and your spiritual habits together form a portrait of what is really valuable to you. Think with me for a moment; if I were to watch with you the video of your last two months, what would I conclude is of true value to you? Or, if I were to watch the last few months of you parenting your kids, what would I say about the level of importance given to this foundational task that God has assigned to you?

I write in *Marriage* that when we talk about values, no passage is more helpful than Matthew 6:19–34. (Why don't you stop and read it right now?) In this passage Jesus uses the word *treasure* to capture the fact that we all live in pursuit of what we've named as important. We are all alike in the fact that we all get up every morning and dig down into the soil of our lives to find some kind of treasure. And the way we speak and behave is our attempt to get out of our lives and relationships the things that are important to us. Now, this is hard to accept, but it needs to be said: parenting is either a thing of the highest treasure to you, and that is demonstrated in your choices, words, and actions every day, or it's not.

So it's humbling but helpful to admit that on this side of our final home, many, many things in our lives as parents compete for a place in the treasure center of our hearts. For example, we live in a world of beautiful physical things, either created by God or crafted by man out of what God created. These physical things play to the quest for beauty that God built inside us, but they can command a place in our hearts that God never intended. And if the pleasure of physical possessions becomes too important for you, it will create all kinds of dysfunction in tasks that God has called you to as a parent. For example, parents who are too controlled by possessions (houses, cars, lawns, furniture, artwork, etc.) tend to be so busy acquiring, maintaining, financing, and protecting their possessions that they have way too little time to invest in their children in the way God intended. Or parents who love possessions too much tend to be so uptight about protecting their possessions that they unwittingly turn their home into an uncomfortable furniture and craft museum that their children are now tasked to live in. It's possible for a mom to be more worried about stains on her couch than the soul of her son, or for a dad to be more focused on the shine and maintenance of his new car than the heart of his daughter. There are parents who fail to be hospitable to the friends of their children because they are concerned about the impact on their physical surroundings and possessions. *Do physical things get in the way of, or create needless tension in, your parenting?*

Or how about success? I am persuaded that the desire for success is another thing that the Creator wired inside us. In the image of the Creator, we're designed to create. We were made to be builders, managers, and doers. We were designed to change our surroundings. We were created to leave an imprint of our work as we move on to another place. We were made to strategize and achieve. Because of all of this achievement, success is important to us. We all want to be successful. In fact, if you have no motivation to succeed anywhere in your life, if you don't care about accomplishing anything, we would all think that something is emotionally or spiritually wrong with you and that you need help. But, like possessions, this very good, God-created thing can become a bad thing in your life if it becomes the ruling treasure it was never meant to be.

Thousands and thousands of children are handed over every day to people they don't know because success in work and career has become too important for their parents. Since neither parent is willing to step away from their work outside the home for fear of its long-term implications on their career and finances, no one is left to take care of the children, so someone else must be hired to do it. I know this is controversial, and I would never judge a couple who have their children in day care without knowing the details of why they made that decision, but I am troubled that we are not talking about this more. I am saddened by the numbers of children who are not with their parents for the bulk of the day during their formative years. I am saddened by the growing cultural comfortability with "latchkey" children. I am concerned about how many exhausted parents pick up their children at the end of their day and are just not able to have the kind of patience and grace that they need for the rest of the evening with their children. This is not a matter of a busy schedule, but busyness that is a matter of values. How many children rarely see their fathers because Dad is off to work before the kids are up and around and home from work after they go to bed? By the time they are teenagers, they are used to Dad not being involved with their lives and don't expect attention or participation from him anymore. *How has the value of career success impacted your commitment to the work that God has called you to as parents?*

Fasten your seatbelts; I'm going to be even more controversial here. I am deeply persuaded that for many people, it is their commitment to ministry that constantly gets in the way of doing what God has called them to do as parents. Perhaps this is the most deceptive treasure temptation of all. There are many, many ministry fathers and mothers who ease their guilty consciences about their inattention and absence by telling themselves that they are doing "the Lord's work." So they accept another speaking engagement, another short-term missions trip, another ministry move, or yet another evening meeting thinking that their values are solidly biblical, when they are consistently neglecting a significant part of what God has called them to. Sadly, their children grow up thinking of Jesus as the one who over and over again took their mom and dad from them.

This is a conversation that parents in ministry need to have and to keep open. It is very interesting that if you listen to people who are preparing couples for a life of ministry, they will warn them about the normal and inescapable tensions between ministry demands and parental calling. But I propose that two observations need to be made here. First, the New Testament never assumes this tension. It never warns you that if you have family and you're called to ministry that you will find yourself in a value catch-22 again and again—that it's nearly impossible to do both well. There is not one warning like this in the Bible. The only thing that gets close to it is that one of the qualifications for an elder is that he must lead his family well. Perhaps this tension is not the result of poor planning on God's part, but because we are seeking to get things out of ministry that we were never meant to get, and because we are, we make bad choices that are harmful to our families. If you get your identity, meaning and purpose, reason for getting up in the morning, and inner peace from your ministry, you are asking your ministry to be your own personal messiah, and because you are, it will be very hard for you to say no, and because it is hard for you to say no, you will tend to neglect important time-relationship commitments you should be making to your children.

But there's one more observation to be considered. The Bible is very clear that God is not so unloving, unwise, unfaithful, and unkind as to call us to one command that will necessitate the breaking of another one of his commands. His commands are not competing demands that flow out of competing value systems. They are a single fabric of threads that, woven together, define what it means to live in a way that is good, right, beautiful, and pleasing to him. Committing yourself to obey one of his commands never means you will suffer and be punished because it has caused you to disobey another. None of his commands exist in isolation and none of them conflict.

So if zeal for ministry causes me to be less than faithful to my calling as a parent in the way that I manage my time and energy, I am seeking to get something out of my ministry that I am not supposed to get. *Do ministry decisions and commitments make it hard for you to faithfully do your work as a parent?*

I would ask you right now to be humble, open, and honest. What competes in your heart and therefore in your daily decisions for the value that parenting should have? In your mundane, repeated, daily schedule does parenting have the place of high honor and high importance that God intended? What other things get in the way? What new and better choices is God calling you to make?

Here's How God Values Parents

The value of parenting goes to the heart of what God has designed every human being to know and to be. To lose this thing is literally to lose a piece of your humanity. Parenting gets to the core of what should motivate every thought, desire, word, decision, or action that every human being has ever taken. There is nothing in the life of any child ever born that is more needed than this. This is the thing that makes parenting of highest importance—*holy* in the true sense of what that word means. This should be the goal at the bottom of all the things you do and all the things you want for your children. To lose sight of this is to miss the point of parenting. To lose sight of this removes the tracks that give direction to all that you do with each of your children. This is the thing that should satisfy you on those good days with your children and keep you motivated on the very hard days with them. This really is the central task that makes your work as a parent a treasure of extreme value. Pay attention to the words below:

> Hear, O Israel; The LORD our God, the LORD is one. You shall love the LORD your God with all your heart and with all your soul and with all your might. And these words that I command you today shall be on your heart. You shall teach them diligently to your children, and shall talk of them when you sit in your house, and when you walk by the way, and when you lie down, and when you rise. You shall bind them as a sign on your hand, and they shall be as frontlets between your eyes. You shall write them on the doorposts of your house and on your gates. (Deut. 6:4–9)

> When your son asks you in time to come, "What is the meaning of the testimonies and the statutes and the rules that the LORD our God has commanded you?" then you shall say to your son, "We were Pharaoh's slaves in Egypt. And the LORD brought us out of Egypt with a mighty hand. And the LORD showed signs and wonders, great and grievous, against Egypt and against Pharaoh and all his household, before our eyes. And he brought us

out from there, that he might bring us in and give us the land that he swore to give our fathers." (Deut. 6:20–23)

There's the value that God places on parenting, summarized in a couple brief, but profound paragraphs. Your work as a parent is a thing of extreme value because God has designed that you would be a principal, consistent, and faithful tool in his hands for the purpose of creating *God-consciousness* and *God-submission* in your children. You can't create this yourself, only God can, but you have been appointed to be an irreplaceable tool in his powerful hands. You see, at the core of what God designed human beings to be is the acknowledgment of his existence and surrender to authority. Those are the things that he meant to rule the heart of everyone who ever lived. Your kids will never be what they're supposed to be or do if they lack God-consciousness. It is the essential thing that must be developed in the heart of every child, and the passages above say that that task was assigned by God to parents.

Your church was not designed to replace you, but to assist and equip you for this essential work. Your government was never designed to replace you, but to protect you as you do this core work. The school near you will never replace you; at the very best it will support you as you do the work that only you can do. You could argue that the chief reason God put parents in children's lives is so that they would know him. The most important thing that a child could ever learn about is the existence, character, and plan of God. If you know this fact, it will alter the way you understand and interpret every other fact in your life.

Now, although God, in grace, has placed you and your children in a physical world that constantly points to him, your children came into the world with a devastating problem. Your children have the perverse and life-shaping ability to look at the world around them and not see God. They will consistently see the signs (the created world), but they will consistently fail to see what the signs point to (the existence and glory of God). And if you don't acknowledge God, not only are you a profoundly disadvantaged human being, but you will then insert yourself in the middle of your world and make it all about you. Children who don't acknowledge God will act as if they are God and will resist the help and rescue that God has provided for them through their parents.

But there is more. At some point your children are going to begin to wonder why they have the rules that they have, why they have been told to believe certain things, and who in the world put you in charge. Sadly, many parents have little more to say than, "Do it because I told you to do it," or "Do it or you're going to get punished." Those explanations get a response from your children only as long as they fear you, but there will come a time when they don't fear you anymore. If all you've given your children is fear of you, then when they leave your home, they will no longer have anything to motivate them to do what is right.

The second paragraph from Deuteronomy 6 helps us here. It tells us that we should root all the rules and beliefs that we give our children not only in the existence of God, but in the things that he has, in grace, done for us. You could say that the advice here is to connect everything you require of your children in behavior and belief to the story of redemption. When your child questions the rules, don't puff up your chest and tell him he better obey or else; talk to him about a loving Redeemer, who not only created him but shed his blood for him so that he could know and do what is right. When your child wonders about what is right and what is wrong, don't just threaten him with the law of God; woo him with the sweet music of the grace of God. When she is struggling with what God says is right, don't talk of God as just a judge, but as a helper and a friend who meets us in our weakness with forgiveness, wisdom, and strength. Blow your child away with God's patience, mercy, and love. Talk again and again about how he willingly exercises his power for our help, benefit, and rescue. Go beyond enforcing your authority and point to his authority, and go beyond pointing to his authority to pointing your children to his grace.

God hasn't made a mistake in tasking you with being his tool for the forming of the souls of your children. You see, he has opened the eyes of your heart to his existence, presence, and rule so that you could be a tool of the same in your children. He has revealed himself to you not just for you but for your children. But there's something else he's done. He's bestowed upon you his forgiving, rescuing, transforming, and delivering grace so that you could be his tool of the same in the lives of each of your children. His gift of grace is not just so that you would be a recipient of grace but also a daily instrument of that very same grace in the lives of those he has placed in your care. In his grace you find everything that you need to be what God wants you to be in the lives of your children and to do what he has called you to do with them.

Here's the bottom line: God has met you so that you would be ready to introduce his glory and grace to your children. Every day is filled with opportunities to point to God, maybe in the fact that water boils, that leaves turn, and that the sun comes up in the morning, or maybe in the power of the storm, the taste of a steak, the beauty of a sunset, or the honey from a bee; all these things exist and are held together only because God created and controls the physical world. God has opened your eyes to his presence and glory so you could help open the eyes of your children. So capture the opportunities around you to point to him. Don't let a day pass without doing it and don't feel that it's weird to talk about God all the time. He is so pictured by his creation that it is positively weird not to be reminded of him and talk about him all the time. And remember, the teenager needs this as much as the toddler does. Nothing is more important in all of life than this; it really is what makes parents so valuable.

There's one more thing that needs to be said; it will be a theme in this book. No one gives grace better than a parent who humbly admits that he desperately needs it himself. Today, with your children, how about being that kind of parent?

2

grace

Principle: God never calls you to a task without giving you what you need to do it. He never sends you without going with you.

MANY, MANY FATHERS AND MOTHERS carry a particular problem into their parenting, and they don't know it. It affects the way they think about the task that has been assigned to them. It affects the way they view their children. It shapes their responses in all the hard moments that parents face. It determines what they will say to themselves as they begin their day or as they crumble into bed, exhausted once again. It leaves many parents feeling unprepared, unable, and discouraged. It causes many parents to wish that they could just quit, when they know in fact they can't. It tempts people to look over the fence and wish that they could have what other parents seem to have, but what seems to have passed them by. It makes parents give in to the temptation to say and do things that they know in their heart of hearts they shouldn't say and shouldn't do.

What is this silent but deadly problem that afflicts so many parents? Way too many Christian parents have a great big, trouble-causing gap in their understanding, celebration of, and reliance upon God's grace. Let me say it now because it will be a theme that will be, in some way, in every chapter of this book. *There is nothing more important to consistent, faithful, patient, loving, and effective parenting than to understand what God has given you in the grace of his Son, the Lord Jesus Christ.* Maybe you're thinking right now, "Paul, I don't need more theology; I need practical help. I believe everything the Bible has to say, but it doesn't seem to have helped my parenting!" I would ask you to open your heart and be patient with me as I explain, because this may be the most important chapter for you in this book. Understanding God's grace will change you, and as it changes you, it will change the way you relate to and parent your children.

It is sad, and a source of so much parenting discouragement and trouble, that so many parents do their work in the middle of a hole in their grasp of God's grace. Most Christian parents have a fairly good understanding of *past grace*, that is, the forgiveness they have received because of the life, death, and resurrection of Jesus, and they have a decent grasp of *future grace*, the place in eternity that is guaranteed them as a child of God. But the problem is that they have little understanding of *present grace*, the right here, right now benefits of the work of Christ for all of us living between the "already" (past grace) and the "not yet" (future grace). Vast numbers of parents think that the phrase "the gospel of God's grace" has nothing to do with the exhaustion they can't seem to shake, or the anger they can't seem to defeat, or the street-level wisdom they feel they lack, or the need for the break they never seem to get. They hear sermons about God's grace and they sing songs about God's grace, but these don't seem to address their struggles as parents. In fact, it seems that what they're getting is anything but grace.

So it needs to be said and then explained that as a child of God, you have been given not only glorious past and future grace, but amazing present grace as well. This grace reaches you wherever God has placed you. This grace reaches you in your darkest parenting moments. This grace addresses your feeling of inability. This grace touches you when you feel you are at the end of your wisdom. This grace is yours for the taking when you're walking down the hallway and you know that you've just blown it. This grace reaches you when your child seems rebellious and hard-hearted and you don't know what to do. This grace touches you in moments of deep parental regret. It gives you a reason to get up in the morning and to be able to sleep at night, no matter what you're facing at the moment. If you would ask me what is the most important thing that God has given you as a parent, I wouldn't say the wisdom principles of his Word. No, I would say, "His grace!" Let me explain why.

Like everything else God calls people to, God doesn't call people to be parents because they are able. If you read your Bible carefully, you will understand that God doesn't call able people to do important things. Abraham wasn't able. Moses wasn't able. Gideon wasn't able. David wasn't able. The disciples weren't able, and the story goes on. The reason for this is that there are no able people out there. They just don't exist. And they surely don't exist as parents. God did not create human beings to be independently able; he designed us to be dependent. It is not a sign of personal weakness or failure of character to feel unable as a parent. The reason you feel this is because it's true! None of us has the natural storehouse of wisdom, strength, patience, mercy, and perseverance that every parent needs in order to do his job well. Independent ability, like independent righteousness, is a delusion. So quit beating yourself up because you feel inadequate; you feel that way because it's true!

Why would a God of perfect wisdom ask inadequate people to do such an important job? The answer is so important to grasp. God calls unable people to do important things because ultimately what he's working on is not your immediate success, but that you would come to know him, to love him, to rest in his grace, and to live for his glory. Let me put it a different way. God calls unable people to do important things so that he will get the glory and not them. He isn't working so that your life as a parent would be easy, predictable, and free from struggle. He calls you to do the impossible so that in your search for help, you would find more than help—you would find him.

Inability doesn't mean that God has made a massive mistake by giving you children, that somehow he's gotten the wrong address and your children would be better off elsewhere. Rather than your inability being in the way of God's plan, it is part of his plan. He knows that parents who admit that they are inadequate and run to God make the best parents. You see, he doesn't ask you to be able; he asks you to be willing. If you are willing, he will meet you in your weakness and change you, and as he changes you, he will work good things through you into the hearts and lives of your children.

But there's something else to be said here. No child really wants to be parented by parents who think that they're able. "Able" parents tend to be proud and self-assured parents. Because they are proud of their ability, they act too quickly and with too much self-confidence, and because they do, they lack patience and understanding. "Able" parents tend to assume that their children should be able too, so they tend to fail to be tender when the weaknesses of their children get exposed. "Able" parents, who pride themselves in keeping the law, tend to give their children more law than grace and are quicker to judge than to understand. And "able" parents tend to want their children to be their trophies, a public demonstration of their ability. It's hard to live with people who deny weakness, because people who deny weakness tend not to be patient, loving, and understanding with people who are weak.

Your inability is not the destruction of your parenting, because God meets people who humbly admit their weaknesses and run to him for help. But your judgments of parental ability may be the very reason you find yourself at odds with children who never seem to measure up to your expectations. "Able" parents seem to be upset when children demonstrate over and over again that what they need is to be parented! If you walk down the hallway mad because your children need correction again, you're mad because at that moment they need what every human being constantly needs: a parent's care. But if you walk down that hallway confessing your need of the Father's care, it is more likely that you will embrace the need of your children for the same care, and you'll be tender as you give it.

God never calls us to a task without giving us what we need to do it. God never sends you into anything without going with you. He never tells you to do something without giving you what you need to do it. This is the story of the whole Bible. This is why God sent his Son to earth. There is only one hero in the Bible; every other character is flawed in some way. God is the hero of every story in the Bible. In fact the Bible is not a collection of stories, but one big story with lots of chapters. It is the story of how God meets weak and failing people with his powerful grace.

What does this have to do with parenting? Everything! It means that if you are God's child, it is impossible for you to be left to your own limited package of resources. It's impossible for you to be relegated to whatever is the size of your strength and wisdom. And here's what you need to remind yourself of every day: God's greatest and most wonderful gift to you as a parent is himself! He knows how hard your task is. He knows that it drives you beyond the borders of your patience and wisdom. He knows that there are times when you feel that you have no clue of what you're doing. He knows there are moments when you wish you could quit and walk away. He knows that there are moments when anger grips you. He knows that your children can get under your skin. He knew what every piece of your struggle would be as a parent, so he knew that the only thing that would help you would be himself. Read these words carefully: "Now to him who is able to do far more abundantly than all we ask or think, according to the power at work within us, to him be glory in the church and in Jesus Christ throughout all generations, forever and ever. Amen" (Eph. 3:20–21).

Here is the single redemptive reality, right here, right now, that makes parenting possible: *God in you*! You read it right. The apostle Paul says that you don't really understand who you are and what you've been given until you understand this amazing thing: that God knew that our calling would be so huge and our weakness so deep that the only thing that would help us was himself. So in an act of incredible grace, he has unbuttoned us and gotten inside of us. Now think about this as a parent. This God who has the ability to do things that are way beyond your ability to conceive, who has perfect wisdom and unlimited strength, right now lives inside of you.

This means that God is with you in the morning when you dread getting out of bed and facing another hard parenting day. He is with you when you have to break up the seventeenth squabble of the morning. He is with you when you have an opening for a very important talk. He is with you when your children are in your face and disrespectful. He is with you when you fall into bed with a combination of exhaustion and regret. He gifts you with his presence. He really does live inside you. You really aren't left to yourself. And he will not turn his back on you until what he has called you to do as a parent is complete.

What do you have as a Christian parent? You have the best thing ever and with it you have hope. You have God in every moment of every day. The question is, Will you remember that you do?

God's grace works to open your eyes to see yourself as a parent accurately. I have to confess that I started out my parenting days as a self-assured, self-righteous parent. I thought I was way more mature than I actually was. I saw myself as a consistent law-keeper and not a law-breaker. I had no idea, as I began, what a negative effect my self-righteousness had on my relationship with my children and the way I handled their weaknesses and failures. If you fall into thinking that you keep God's law perfectly (although few people consciously say that to themselves), then you expect the people around you to do the same. Self-righteous people find it all too easy to judge and condemn people who are not measuring up to the standard that they assess they are keeping.

So here's what God does in all of our lives. He uses things like our marriages and our parenting to expose our hearts to us. He used parenting to expose thoughts, attitudes, and desires in my heart that I had previously denied were there. It was my struggle with irritation, impatience, anger, and lack of gentleness and joy as a dad that God used to show me how far I still fell beneath his standard and how much I still needed his forgiving and transforming grace.

Here's the humbling conclusion that God, in grace, led me to: *I am more like my children than unlike them*—and so are you. The reality is that there are few struggles in the lives of my children that aren't in my life as well (materialism, relationships, wanting my own way, attraction to the world, subtle idolatries, etc.). This admission transformed my parenting. Instead of approaching them with self-righteous outrage, I moved toward them as a sinner in need of grace needing to confront a sinner in need of grace. God's plan is to make his invisible grace visible to children by sending parents of grace to give grace to children who need grace. And parents who know they need grace tend to want to give grace to children who are just like them.

God's grace frees you from having to deny your weaknesses. I love the fact that biblical faith never requires that you deny reality. If you have to deny reality to feel good about your life, you may have temporary peace, but you're not exercising biblical faith. The Bible is a shockingly honest book that shows us the blood, dirt, and smoke of life in a fallen world. Yet the Bible is the most hopeful of any book ever written because of the transformative power of the life, death, and resurrection of Jesus. Here's what this means for you as a parent: God never asks you to act as a parent as if you're something that you're not. In fact, he does just the opposite. God welcomes you to look at yourself in the heart- and life-exposing mirror of his Word to see yourself as you really are and to be willing to confess your faults to those around you. And here's why you can have the courage to live this way: as a parent you do not ever need to fear knowing yourself, you do not have to fear being known by those around you, and you do not have to fear being exposed as less than perfect because there is nothing that could ever be known or exposed about you as a parent that hasn't already been covered by the blood of Jesus.

It never works, as a mom or dad, to act as if you're more righteous than you are. The fact of the matter is that your children will get to know the real you. They will come to see your spiritual and character weaknesses, and if you deny these, you will embitter your children. But if you are a parent who quickly confesses wrong to your children, you will endear yourself to them and present yourself as someone who will be approachable when they have failed. Humble, confessing parents encourage their children to be humble and confessing too, and the result is that they have many opportunities to talk about the rescuing love of Jesus.

God's grace rescues you from you. When you are frustrated, mad, discouraged, unkind, abusive, bitter, joyless, vengeful, or irritated as a parent, you don't so much need to be rescued from your children—you need to be rescued from you.

Pretend that I have a bowl of water in my hands and I shake it vigorously and water splashes out of the bowl. And suppose I ask you why water spilled out of the bowl, and you answer that it spilled because I shook it. It all sound pretty logical, doesn't it? But the answer is only partially correct. Why did water splash out of the bowl? Because water was in the bowl. If the bowl had been filled with milk, you could shake it for an eternity and water would never spill out of it. In the same way it is very important for parents to understand and humbly admit that when we are shaken by the sin, weakness, rebellion, foolishness, or failure of our children, what comes out of us (words, actions, attitudes) is what is already inside us.

This means that my biggest, ongoing problem as a dad is not my children, it's me. My children don't cause me to do and say what I do and say. No, the cause of my actions is found inside my own heart. My children are simply the occasion where my heart reveals itself in words and actions. So I need much more than just rescue and relief from my children; I need rescue from me. This is why Jesus came, to provide us with the rescue that we all need but that we cannot provide for ourselves.

If you blame your children for your bad attitudes, actions, and words, not only will you embitter them, but in blaming them, you will fail to reach out for the help that is yours in the rescuing, forgiving, and transforming grace of Jesus. And because you shift the blame, you will fail to grow as a parent and you will repeat the same patterns over and over again. When you are willing to confess that you're the biggest problem in your parenting, you are on the road to very good things in you and in your work with your kids.

God's grace grows and changes you as a parent. I hinted at this above, but I want to say more. Because you and I always do our parenting between the "already" of our conversion and the "not yet" of our final destination, we parent in the middle of our own sanctification. Remember the gospel; although the *power* of sin has been broken in the beautiful justifying mercies of Jesus Christ, the *presence* of sin still remains with us. So God's present zeal is to progressively deliver us from the remaining hold that sin has on us. This means that he will use the pressures, opportunities, hassles, burdens, griefs, temptations, and joys to grow and change us.

Think about how beautiful this is. In every moment as you are parenting your children, the heavenly Father is parenting you. As you are lovingly confronting your children with the hope that they would confess their need and commit to change, the heavenly Father is confronting you. As you seek to encourage your children toward what is right, your Father in heaven is working to grow the desire for right in you. In all those moments when you intervene to protect your children from their own foolish choices, the great Father is protecting you from you.

Here's what you and I should never forget. As we seek to parent our children, the heavenly Father is parenting everyone in the room. Like our children, we need to grow and mature. Like our children, we haven't progressed beyond the need for a Father's care. Like our children, we need a parent who will not turn his back on us even though we stumble and fall again and again.

God hasn't just sent you to do his work in the lives of your children; he will use the lives of your children to advance his work in you. How about being a parent who admits the need to be parented? Thankfully the Bible promises, "As a father shows compassion to his children, so the LORD shows compassion to those who fear him" (Ps. 103:13).

God's grace works to make your heart tender. Do you think about, speak to, and act toward your children out of a tender heart? If your children could describe you accurately, would *tenderness* be one of the terms they would use? Has parenting pushed you toward patient gentleness or impatient harshness? Remember, your words and actions are always an accurate reflection of the true condition of your heart. The things you do and say always tell you more about yourself than whoever you're speaking or responding to.

I am deeply persuaded that there are many hard-hearted parents who have no idea that they parent out of a hardened heart. Think of what the word picture "hard heart" describes. If I had a stone in my hands and I squeezed it with all my might, what would happen? The answer is nothing. Stone is hard and therefore resistant to change. It is not malleable; you can press it again and again and it will not change. Hard-hearted parents think that they are right and okay, and because they do, they don't feel the need to change and grow. So they tend to repeat the same bad patterns again and again. This sets up unnecessary tension with their children because as they are requiring their children to change, they are not holding themselves to the same standard. So they'll yell at their children to stop yelling, but fail to confess that they yell when they shouldn't. They'll demand that their children stop fighting, but they'll fight with their children about things that aren't important. They'll require their children to be kind, while they permit themselves to speak and act toward their children in ways that are unkind. Children begin to lose respect for the parent who is content with a "do what I say and not as I do" relationship to children.

God will use the hammer of his grace to tenderize us, so that we will be part of what he is seeking to do in our children and not stand in the way of it. The difficulties you face as a parent are not signs that God has forgotten you, but are the tenderizing mercies of a loving and faithful father. He is softening your heart so you can be a tool of heart change in the lives of those he's placed in your care.

God's grace liberates you from the prison of regret. One of the most beautiful things about God's grace is that it welcomes you to fresh starts and new beginnings. Way too many parents are paralyzed by a whole catalog of "what ifs" and "if onlys." Yes, you will make mistakes. Yes, you will learn and grow as a parent. Yes, you will understand parenting more with your last child than you did your first child. Yes, you will look back and be embarrassed by things you said and things you did. Yes, you will do some of the things your parents did that you swore you'd never do. Yes, as your children grow up, they will remind you of some of the painful things you did in the early years. Yes, you will wish that you had known more sooner. If you're at all humble as a parent, you will look back with some regret.

But it's important to understand that although regret is a sign of a humble heart, it is dangerous and debilitating to live in regret. Living in regret robs you of your confidence. Living in regret renders you timid. Living in regret kidnaps your courage. Living in regret weakens or steals your hope. Living in regret drags the past into the present. Living in regret even drags the past into the future. And for all of its remembering, regret can be tragically forgetful. What is it that regret tends to forget? Regret tends to forget the cross of the Lord Jesus Christ. On the cross, Jesus bore the entire burden of our guilt and our shame. On the cross, Jesus purchased, by the shedding of his blood, our complete forgiveness: past, present, and future. This means that we can boldly come to him in our failure, receive his forgiveness, deposit our regret at his feet, and move on to new and better ways of doing what he has called us to do as parents.

The issue here is not whether you remember the mistakes of your past days of parenting. This issue is, are you emotionally and spiritually paralyzed by them in a way that makes it hard for you to do what God is calling you to do in the present? God's grace welcomes you to learn from your past, to confess your faults, receive forgiveness, lay down your burden of guilt and shame, and with new hope and courage give yourself with joy to what God is calling you to as a parent right here, right now.

God has called you to be a parent. How does he give you what you need for this calling? He gives you what you need by giving you *himself*, and in giving you himself, he showers his amazing, forgiving, rescuing, transforming, empowering, and wisdom-giving grace down on you. As you parent today, you are invited to remember that you are not alone in your house with your children. Someone else walks the hallways and stands in the family room with you. Someone rides in the van with you on the way to yet another scary trip with your kids to the mall. Someone walks with you as you enter your teenager's room to confront him about something he did. Someone is with you as you relive the events of the day before you fall asleep, preparing to face another parenting day. Someone is with you as you get up, already exhausted as usual, before the sun rises. The one who called you to this very important job is with you and because he is, there's hope. Sure, there will be times when you'll find yourself at the end of your rope, but fight fear and discouragement with expectancy; your Savior's rope never ends, and he will never leave you alone!

3

LAW

Principle: Your children need God's law, but you cannot ask the law to do what only grace can accomplish.

THEY WERE SO DISHEARTENED. They thought they had done exactly what God called them to do. They had faithfully exercised their authority. They had made the rules clear and the threat of punishment obvious. They had followed through again and again. They didn't compromise, no matter where they were and no matter what the situation was. They told their children again and again that they did what they did as parents because it was what God commanded them to do. They told their children repeatedly that no matter how old they got, they would still have to obey somebody's rules.

Now they were wondering if it was all worth it. They were plagued with the question of what had gone wrong. Josh was sixteen and as rebellious as they come. He seemed in love with the world and everything in it. Rules to him weren't things to be obeyed; they were challenges to be accepted. He fought every regulation with mocking disrespect. He acted as if he hated his mom and dad, saying things to them that were intended to hurt. He'd told them a thousand times that he couldn't wait to get out of their house and be on his own, then he'd make his own choices and there was nothing they could do about it. He really did seem to be a person who loved evil and hated what is good.

Sitting on her nightly perch outside Josh's bedroom door, as she did every night, to keep him from sneaking out, she recounted the years. She thought about that sweet little boy that everyone liked, contrasted with the angry young man behind the door. She felt disappointed, humiliated, and powerless. She was tired and secretly couldn't wait for him to leave for good.

Jessica was the typical, busy little three-year-old. Life was her playground, and she seemed to get up every morning to enjoy every part of it. Sally was increasingly tired of chasing her around the house as she proceeded to get into everything. She felt that Jessica didn't listen to her. A couple months ago she'd tried counting. "Jessica, get out of that drawer, 1 . . . 2 . . . 3." You know the drill: the threat was that at "3," Mom would swoop in, and you didn't want to know what would happen next. But Jessica had survived many 3s, and nothing terrible had happened. Sally was now at 5 and getting almost no response from Jessica. Threat was no longer a threat. In fact, counting had sadly become an invitation for Jessica to do whatever wrong she was doing for a little longer. She knew she could push her mommy just a little bit further. And Sally was tired of counting, and with each larger number she felt herself getting angrier and more discouraged. Counting didn't work, and she couldn't figure out what else to do.

Frank and Mary were so worried about Emma. It wasn't that she was hard to live with; on the contrary, she was always friendly and polite. In many ways, Emma was the dream teenager. She did well in high school and as a junior was already getting scholarship offers from prestigious universities. She participated in her youth ministry without resistance and volunteered with Habitat for Humanity. From a distance it all looked good.

But Frank and Mary knew it was not good. Emma spent more and more time on Facebook, Instagram, and Twitter. She was obsessed with the lives of the current pop stars and young actors. Every day she read every trashy gossip website there was. She was also obsessed with fashion, with how she looked and how people responded to how she looked. Emma couldn't bear not having a boyfriend and had begun to dress more provocatively. The faith, which she had never rejected outright, seemed less and less important to her. She worshiped every day at the feet of all of the current idols of the surrounding culture, but she didn't know it was worship. Frank and Mary felt they were losing her, but didn't know how to handle it. Emma was not rebellious; she was responsible with her school work and basically obeyed the rules at home. Whenever Frank and Mary expressed their concern to Emma, she would tell them that they were just old-fashioned and needed to relax, everything was okay. But Emma was being captured; her parents saw it, but no rule they laid down seemed to rescue her.

Rob was a quiet kid. He spent a lot of time alone, and he didn't seem to mind it. He loved to skateboard, but didn't have much time for, or interest in, organized sports. He was not hard to parent, except that he played it very close to the chest. It was always hard to get Rob to open up and talk about anything personal, so his mom and dad felt that the older he got, the less they knew him. His senior year he became very close to a friend at his high school. They began to spend hour upon hour together, both inside and outside the home. It was not at all unusual for Rob and his friend to spend the weekend at one another's house.

For several weeks Rob's mom had wondered if something was wrong with Rob. He just didn't seem like himself, but when she would inquire, Rob would say it was nothing, that he was cool. Finally, one night, when his dad was away on a business trip, his mom cornered him, putting on the pressure for him to tell her what was wrong. He resisted for a while, but she would not give up, and with more emotion than he had displayed in a long time, Rob said, "I'm in love." His mom said, "Well, you don't have to be embarrassed or fearful about that." But Rob said, "I'm in love with Nate [his friend from school]." Holding on to her emotions, his mom said, "What do you mean when you say you're 'in love' with Nate?" Rob said, "Mom, I'm gay, and I knew if I told you that you and dad would hate me, but it's true, I'm gay, and there's nothing or no one that can do anything about it." With that he stormed out of the room.

Although Rob's mom and dad had expressed their love for him no matter what, it wasn't long before they had constructed and announced a whole new set of regulations for Rob. He had to surrender his car keys, he was no longer allowed to see Nate, he had to put a content limiter on his computer, he had to leave his bedroom door open when he was home, and he had a new, earlier curfew. Rob grew more and more sullen and angry, and he and Nate continued to find ways to be with one another.

A Subtle but Foundational Mistake

One theme runs through each of these stories, an error that each of these loving and well-meaning parents is making. Did you see it? Consider that every parent puts their confidence in something. Every parent knows that their children have to grow, mature, and change. As a parent you know that it is your job to help form character (obedience, respect, honesty, willingness, etc.) in your children. So as a parent, you will rely on something to create change in your children. There is some tool that you will use again and again in the belief that it has the power to change your child. And because you have confidence in that tool, you will use it again and again, in situation after situation and with child after child. The change tool that you have placed your confidence in will not only be the tool that you reach for when change is indicated, but it will also be the lens you'll look through to assess situations and to evaluate your children.

Let me stop right now and get you to examine your parenting. If I watched the last six weeks of your parenting, how you evaluate your children and seek to work change in them, what would I conclude is the primary tool that you're relying on? Don't answer quickly. Scan what you've done with your children over the last several weeks. Could it be that you are making the same mistake the parents in my stories are making? Could it be that your primary tool of change doesn't have the power to do what you're asking it to do? Could it be that the evidence is right in front of you, but you don't see it? Could it be that there is a new, a better way that you believe in, but that hasn't influenced your parenting?

Now, read what I'm about to write very carefully. I am convinced that without knowing it, thousands and thousands of well-meaning Christian parents are asking the law to do in the lives of their children what only the powerful grace of God can accomplish. This truth needs to be considered and needs to shape everything you do as a parent: *If rules and regulations had the power to change the heart and life of your child, rescuing your child from himself and giving him a heart of submission and faith, Jesus would have never needed to come!* You see, what you assign the power of change to will then shape the way you parent your children in all of those mundane and not-so-mundane moments that end up forming who they are as they leave your home. Let me explain.

Law and Grace

Your Children Need God's Law

Check out the words of the apostle Paul: "What shall we then say? That the law is sin? By no means! Yet if it had not been for the law, I would not have known sin. For I would not have known what it is to covet if the law had not said, 'You shall not covet'" (Rom. 7:7). Our children are born with a desperate need for God's law. Because they come into the world as fools, not knowing what is true or what is false, what is good or what is bad, what is right or what is wrong, they need the *grace of wisdom* that God's law alone can give. Apart from God's law human beings wouldn't have a clue how they are supposed to think, what they are supposed to desire, how they are supposed to speak, or how they were designed to behave. Like all human beings, children were not made to be self-governing, that is, to be guided by independent thoughts and desires. Children need to be given tracks to run on and boundaries to stay inside of. So God in his wonderful mercy gives us his law so that our behavior would be guided by a clear knowledge of what is right and wrong. But the guidance of the law is meant to do something else. It is meant to protect your child from herself. All children come into the world as sinners. This means all children are a danger to themselves and need the protection that God's law gives. Because God's law provides your children with guiding and protecting wisdom that they would not have without it, his law is good for them.

But there is another way that God's law is good for your children; it provides them with the *grace of conviction*. Your children would have no idea that they are sinners in need of protection, wisdom, forgiveness, and rescue without the standard of God's law. You know how it works: it's only when you apply a standard of measurement to a board that you realize you have cut it too short. One of the most dangerous things in your child's life is his blindness to the depth of his spiritual need. A child who does not see himself clearly will resist his parents' wisdom, guidance, discipline, and correction. Why? Because he doesn't think he needs it. The law is very good at exposing not only our behavior, but our hearts as well. God's law is the ultimate human measuring system, and because it is, it's good for your children to be regularly exposed to it and exposed by it.

Your Children Need to Understand the Law's Weakness

Yes, your children need the law of God in their lives, but it is very dangerous as parents to daily ask the law to do what only grace can accomplish. I am afraid that many, many Christian parents do exactly that without knowing it. They have reduced Christian parenting down to being a really faithful lawgiver, arresting officer, prosecutor, judge, and jailer. So their parenting is basically a body of rules followed by threats of punishment. Yes, children need rules and they need faithful correction, but that simply is not enough. Think with me. If all that your children needed was the knowledge and enforcement of rules, as I wrote earlier, then the life, death, and resurrection of Jesus would not have been necessary. Jesus came because the law was good, but definitely not enough to solve the great human dilemma of sin. Remember, the greatest danger to your child is not the evil outside them; it's the sin inside them that is the greatest of all threats to their well-being.

This is what every parent of every child needs to understand: the law does a very good job of exposing your child's sin, but it has no power whatsoever to deliver your child from it. The law has no ability to rescue your child from the power of sin's grip. The law has no ability to give your child a new heart. The law has no ability to create the lasting change in your child that every parent longs for. The law cannot and will not rescue, redeem, and restore your child, but that's exactly what every child needs. So if you are going to be a tool of change in God's hands in the lives of your children, you need more than God's law in your personal parenting toolbox.

But there's something else I need to say here. It's not just that as parents we tend to put all the eggs of our hope for our children in the basket of the law, but we also tend to replace God's perfect law with a sorry human second best. Somehow, someway God's law gets replaced by our law—a law that's sadly driven by our craving for affirmation, control, peace, success, and reputation. So we make selfish, impatient, and angry demands on our children, treating them as indentured servants who exist to lessen our load of daily chores and to make our lives more comfortable. The fact is that our children weren't created and given to us for our sake, but for God's sake and their good.

So we get mad at our kids, not first because they're breaking God's law but because they're in the way of our law (something that we want). Think of how little of your anger as a parent in the last few months had anything at all to do with God's law. It's not just *law dependency* that keeps us from doing all we should do as God's representatives in the lives of our children, but it's *law replacement* that causes us to do all kinds of things we shouldn't do toward them. The good news is that there really is a new and better way for us and for our children.

You Need to Understand That God's Grace Is Essential

I think we would be shocked if we knew how many homes of parents who love to sing of God's grace on Sunday completely forget that grace as they parent their children the rest of the week. But without the intervention of God's grace, your children will not be who they are supposed to be or do what they are supposed to do. Remember, it's the sin inside them that messes everything up. It's sin that makes your children resist your guidance and authority. It's sin that causes children to constantly be in conflict with their siblings. It's sin that gets in the way of your child's learning in school. It's sin that causes children to be attracted to what is hurtful or destructive. It's sin that causes your children to be entitled, demanding, materialistic, and complaining. It's sin that causes your children to act as if they are the center of the universe and that life should do their bidding. It's sin that causes children to say hurtful things to their parents, siblings, and peers. And it's sin that makes parenting difficult, demanding, and exhausting.

The law has no ability to deliver your children from this mess— the very mess that you have to deal with every day as a parent. So your children came into the world in desperate need of God's rescuing, forgiving, transforming, and delivering grace. You could argue that it's God's grace that is the only hope for parents and children alike. As a parent, you are not called to just enforce God's law in the lives of your children, but also to constantly exhibit and teach God's grace to them as well.

But I have to remind you that you need that grace as much as your children do. If you are ever going to function as God's ambassador, you need to be rescued by powerful grace from your bondage to you. As parents we need to be rescued from our addiction to the law of our comfort, pleasure, success, and control. It's not our children's sin that is in the way of good parenting; it's our tendency to make parenting about our little kingdom of wants, needs, and desires, and our tendency to want our children to serve the purposes of our kingdom rather than submit to the purposes of God's kingdom.

I make the best cinnamon rolls in the universe. Sorry, there's just no doubt about it. It's one of the things I like to do on our family vacations. And when I make them, I know what's going to happen. That gorgeous smell will pull my children out of bed and down the hallway. They will bow at my feet and say, "Our life is good because we have a father who makes cinnamon rolls!"

So it's early in the morning, I am the only one up, and I am making the rolls, thinking about the delight to follow. Finally they're in the oven, and the house is beginning to be enveloped in the beautiful smell. I position myself on a chair that looks down the hallway, anticipating the worship that is to come. One of my sons appears and instead of praising my existence, he says these shocking words: "Dad, can I make something else for breakfast?" I want to say, "Are you an idiot? Of course you can't make something else! Why in the world would you?" But I hold my tongue as he explains that his wife (interloper in the family that she is) doesn't like to eat sweet things for breakfast, so he's going to make some scrambled eggs. Eggs! Eggs! Beaten up former embryos!

I know I shouldn't be angry, but I am. I know this isn't personal, but to me it is! Now we're at the breakfast table, and my son's wife positions herself right in front of that big pile of cinnamon-oozing wonderfulness. I know she will break down and take one, but she doesn't. Every bite of those eggs bothers me. I know scrambled eggs are soft, but I think I can hear her chewing and it drives me crazy. I can't believe she's rejected my transcendent rolls for her eggs!

Now think of what that whole scene is driven by. God's existence and his law are out the window. It is all about me. The law of my self-centered expectations for my children. The law of my acclaim, my comfort, and my appreciation. I propose that so much of what drives our responses to our kids is an unannounced set of laws that are more about what we want for ourselves and our lives than what God wants for and from our children. In our allegiance to our law, we end up breaking God's law in our interactions with our children. In this way we are just like our children: people who need to be rescued from ourselves.

You Need to Preach the Gospel to Your Children

I don't mean that parents should "preach" to their children in the Sunday-morning-sermon style. I mean you should look every day for every opportunity to point your needy kids to the presence, promises, power, and grace of Jesus. Now here's where I think this parental mission of grace begins. It doesn't begin with your concern for the deep spiritual needs of your children, but rather with a humble admission of the depth of your own need. It is when you confess that you don't have a prayer of being what God wants you to be and doing what God wants you to do as a parent without the rescuing and enabling grace of God. You become increasingly excited about and thankful for the rescue, and your personal thankfulness causes you to be enthusiastic about your children reaching out for the same kind of help.

Parents, we all need to have an "everything I do, I do to point my children to the presence and promises of God's grace" way of parenting our children. Every conversation is an opportunity. Pointing them to the beauty of nature is an opportunity, every moment of correction and discipline is an opportunity, every sibling battle is an opportunity, success or failure at school is an opportunity, family worship is an opportunity, birthdays and holidays provide an opportunity, teenage identity angst is an opportunity, bedtime conversations provide an opportunity, discussions after watching something on Netflix provide an opportunity.

There will be no want of opportunities to talk to your children about their inescapable need for God's grace. There will be no lack of opportunity for telling the story of how Jesus meets those needs. Because, by God's plan, every good thing, every beautiful thing, every hard thing, every sad thing, and everything to celebrate gives us an opportunity to point to the God who, in grace, rules it all. The question is: will you see those opportunities in the mundane moments of parenting and capture them again and again and again?

What *do* you want for your children? Do you just want them to buck up and obey? Do you just want to be able to control their behavior until they're out of your care? Do you want little more than children who do what they're told and don't embarrass you in public? Or do you long for more—much, much more? Do you want children who live every day as God designed them to live, whose hearts are ruled by worship of him and who gladly live inside his boundaries? You know, in your heart of hearts, you can't produce children like this on your own. If you've paid attention, you've begun to realize that you can't control the hearts of your children even with the best lectures, the best correction, and the most faithful discipline.

So it's time to give up trying to do in the hearts and lives of your children what only God can do. It's time for you to surrender your heart to his grace and lead the hearts of your children to trust in his grace. You say, "Paul, I get it, but I just don't know practically what that looks like." Well, I'm happy to say that this is what the rest of this book is about.

You Need to Model the Gospel of Grace to Your Children

I know what raising children was like for me, and I suspect it is this way for you as well. If as parents we really are called to be visible ambassadors of the presence, character, and plan of God in the lives of our children, then I often did a very poor job. In the way I often reacted to my children, I presented God as an irritable, impatient, judgmental, loud, and accusatory father. There were themes of daily contradiction between the message of grace that I talked to my kids about and the lack of grace that shaped my responses to them. I often failed to model the stunning patience and beauty of that grace. I was committed to what was right for my children, but I went at it in the wrong way. "I can't believe that you would do such a thing!" "I do and do for you, and this is the thanks I get!" "You don't want to know what's going to happen if I have to come up those stairs one more time!" "Would you just be quiet for one meal so I can for once eat in peace?"

No child hears that kind of talk and says to himself, "What a wise and loving parent! I know I can share my heart with this person. I just wish he would say more of these things to me! I am so thankful that this person is my parent! I think I'm beginning to see my heart." No one, adult or child, has ever had someone get up into their face and yell at them and has walked away feeling helped by it. All we just want is to escape, to have it end.

If God's plan really is to make his invisible grace visible by sending parents of grace to give grace to children who desperately need grace, then I am called not just to preach that grace but to live and model it for my children every day. Writing this makes me weak in my knees, because I know this is counterintuitive to me and to you. As parents we lose our way, and we want our own way; we forget God's plan and follow our own plan. If we are ever to represent the great Father well, we need to be fathered by him as well. If we are going to give grace to our children, we need to confess that we are but children in daily need of the Father's care. If we are going to be patient, we need to confess our need for patience. If we are going to be forgiving, we need to admit our need for forgiveness. If we are going to persevere, we need to humbly admit that our only hope is that our heavenly Father will never give up on us. And if we are going to teach our children to run to Jesus daily, we must run to Jesus daily as well. If we want our children to be sad in the face of the sin of their hearts and hands, we must mourn our sin as parents as well.

You see, it is only as we are willing to confess that we are more like than unlike our children, that we ourselves need parenting every day, that we will be parents in need of a father's grace who will again and again lead our children to the grace of the Father.

4

inability

Principle: Recognizing what you are unable to do is essential to good parenting.

IT WAS A PUBLIC SCENE. If you were near, it was impossible not to stop whatever you were doing and look and listen. And for me it was impossible not to wonder how many times that same scene was repeated by parents that same day, who meant well, but who had lost their way. I know the belief that was behind what that mother did in the mall that day. I know that belief because in my earlier parenting days I bought into it too. In her heart of hearts that mom felt she was being a good and faithful parent, that she was doing exactly what a parent should do in that situation. And I don't doubt her motives, but what she did was propelled by something that many parents believe, but that is dead wrong.

Unaware of those of us around her, she hurled accusations and threats at her little boy. Her face was stern and her voice was loud, and she just knew that talk would change that little boy. She knew that what he did, he would never be so bold as to do again. She was letting him have it, and she believed that letting him have it would change him. He quietly cried as she was so up in his face that I'm sure he could not only hear her words, but feel her breath. Yes, he would remember his mom's anger, but I'm not so sure that anger would do what was intended. She grabbed his hand and walked away, still making her point as he dragged on behind her.

Do I think that that mom loved her little boy? Yes, I think she probably did. But the way she parented him was shaped by buying into something that just won't ever work.

Powerless

You may be wondering what the title for this section of this chapter has to do with the story you just read. That mother was in her son's face with threatening anger because she assigned to herself power that she doesn't have. I've bought into this delusion. I've heard parents verbalize it. "If it's the last thing I do, I'll get my children to believe." "I will discipline the hell out of my children." "It's my job to ensure that they do what is right." "If I do nothing else, I will send children out into the world who are prepared to live right." "After I'm done with him, he'll never even think of doing that again." The assessment in these statements that children need to change is right. The deep desire for that change which motivates a parent is right. The commitment to work for that change is right. Then what is wrong with each of these statements? Each of them assumes power on the part of parents that no parent has, and that assumption creates all kinds of parenting trouble.

If you are going to be what God has designed you to be as a parent and do what he's called you to do, you must confess one essential thing. This confession has the power to change much about the way you act and react toward your children. It is vital that you believe and admit that *you have no power whatsoever to change your child.* Now think again from the perspective of the gospel of Jesus Christ, which is the central theme of the book that is our most reliable parenting guide. If any human being possessed the power to create lasting change in any other human being, again, Jesus would not have had to come! The incarnation, life, death, and resurrection of Jesus stand as clear historical evidence that human power for change does not exist. The reason God went to such an extreme and elaborate extent in controlling the events of history so that at just the right time his Son would come and do for us what we could not do ourselves, is because there was no other way.

Parenting is not about *exercising power for change* in your children. Parenting is about your humble faithfulness in being willing to *participate in God's work of change* for the sake of your children. Parents, here's what you need to understand: God has given you *authority* for the work of change, but has not granted you the *power* to make that change happen. But we buy into the delusion of thinking again and again that that power is ours. We think that if we speak just a little bit louder, or stand a little bit closer, or make the threat a little bit scarier, or the punishment a little more severe, then our children will change. And because the change doesn't happen, we tend to bring it on even stronger.

Oh, sure, you can scare or reward your children into temporary change. You can temporarily buy them off or scare them off. You can exercise temporary control over a child's behavior, but what needs to change in order for that change to last and bear fruit is something inside the child. Let me say it this way: the behavior of your children is symptomatic of what is going on inside your children. Inside change always precedes lasting outside change. In parenting, what you are dealing with is way deeper than the need for behavioral change. What you're always dealing with is the need for heart change, and we simply have no power at all to change another person's heart. (If you want to know more about that, there is a chapter coming dedicated to that discussion.)

Now here's the point: if as a parent you think that you have power that you don't have, you will do things that you should not do and you will fail to do things that are vital to do. When you think your job is to change your child and you've been given the power to do it, your parenting will tend to be demanding, aggressive, threatening, and focused on rules and punishments. In this kind of parenting you are working to make your children into something rather than working to help them to see something and seek something. In this form of parenting, it is all about *you and your children*, rather than you being an *agent of what only God can do in your children*. Your hope is that you will exercise the right power, at the right time, and in the right way so change in your children will result. That process is profoundly different than working to be a useful tool in the hands of a God of glorious transforming grace, who alone is your hope and the hope of your children.

Here's the bottom line for every parent: the change that has to happen in each of your children, you can't create. In fact, nowhere in his Word has God tasked you with the responsibility to create it. Good parenting is about becoming okay with the fact that you are powerless to change your child. In fact, good parenting is about celebrating the fact that God has never and will never put the burden of change on you. Because changing your children is a burden that we could never bear, God bore that burden for us by sending his Son to be the author of lasting personal change. The burden that caused his death liberates us parents and gives new life to our children. Now that's good news! So our job is simple; it's not to create change, but to be humble and willing instruments of change in the hands of the one and only author of change.

This means that you and I have to be willing to let go of those old, human-power parenting habits. We have to stop with the loud voices, the escalating threats, the subtle name calling, words of condemnation, ever-worsening punishments, telling our children how much more righteous we are than they, the silent treatment, and withholding affection when they've upset us. Don't get me wrong here. Your children do need you to exercise authority, but not as the creator of change. They need you to exercise authority as the representative of the author of all lasting change. This means that you quit trying to exercise whatever power is available to you to get your children to change and begin to think as a representative. Representing the God who gives us grace for change means looking for daily opportunities to communicate that grace, helping our children to see how they need that grace, and modeling that grace in the way that we speak and act toward our children.

Now in case you're wondering, I'm not talking about forsaking your authority as a parent. I'm not talking about letting your children do whatever they want to do. I'm not talking about parenting that has no correction or discipline. I'm not talking about ignoring the wrong things that your children do or ever calling wrong right. What I'm talking about is the exercise of parenting authority that submits to the essential power of transforming grace. This kind of authority abandons hope in human power and gladly places its hope in the awesome power of God. His power alone is the hope of every parent and every child whether they know it or not. You don't get up every morning and shoulder again the burden of your children's change; rather, you get up and surrender everything that you will do and say that day to the God of change who has sent you to be his representative.

Power Tools

Let me point you to the three most often used tools of parental power that we tend to use to create change in our children.

Fear

The power that we buy into here is that we can issue a big enough threat that creates a big enough fear to change our kids. So every day with our children is marked by threats like this: "You do not want to know what's going to happen if I have come up these steps one more time. I will be on the news! 'Father disciplines his children, pictures and details on the news at ten o'clock.'" Or like this: "You clean up your room and fast or I'll empty it of everything but a mattress and a pillow. Then you can sleep on the floor and think about how sloppy you are and about all the things that you used to have that have been taken away." And like this: "You do that again and you'll be grounded for months. I'll ground you so long, you'll forget what the outside looks like!"

Why do we use threats? Because they're temporarily effective. Think about it: when you're a full-grown adult and your child is half your size, you are a threatening presence. Your bulging eyes, red face, pointed finger, and loud voice are threatening. You can do things that will make your child afraid to cross you, but a distinction needs to be made here. Having a child that has enough experience of what happens when you get angry, to make him afraid to cross you, is profoundly different from having a child who is motivated by an internal desire to do what is right and a knowledge that he needs God's help in order to do it.

The first child has not changed at all; he's simply trying to avoid your threats. If you would remove the threats or if he would discover how to disobey without you knowing it, he would go right back to the behaviors you have prohibited. Your threats haven't stimulated internal change; rather, your threats are a system of external control. Remember that you represent the ultimate Father, who is not satisfied with using his power to just control us. He exercised his rule by sending his Son to radically rescue and transform us. Yes, he does put holy threats before us, but it is dramatically clear in Scripture that if all we needed were a list of divine threats, again, the life, death, and resurrection of Jesus would not have been necessary.

I need to make another observation about the power of threats. I've experienced what I'm about to say, and I've talked to many parents who have experienced it as well. There comes a time in the life of all children when they are no longer threatened by their parents. If you've depended on threats to control your kids, the moment that I'm now talking about is both scary and depressing, because the tool that you've used for years suddenly doesn't work. I have four children. I'm about 5'10", and my shortest child is my daughter and she's about 6'1". She has three taller brothers. I ended my parenting days, when our children were still in our home, by looking up to talk to my kids. If your children are physically taller than you and way less dependent on you than they once were, you are no longer a threatening presence. Once your kids begin to be your intellectual and physical peers, they stop being threatened by you.

Threat without grace is a tool of external control that will fail to change your son or daughter in the foundational way that every child needs to be changed.

Reward

This may be the most popular way we fight our inability to change our children. We manipulate them to do what we want them to do by holding certain rewards in front of them. This strategy should not be confused with God's righteous work of motivating our obedience by the promise of spiritual reward. Instead, we find something that our child really wants, and we hold it out and say, "If you do _____ I will give you _____."

Josh is eleven years old and is not getting along very well with his seven-year-old sister, Mary. Mary is often left crying after one of her encounters with her older brother. Josh's parents have become increasingly frustrated and discouraged because this has become a daily occurrence. So Josh's dad comes to him and says, "Josh, you know that little drone that you've been looking at on the Internet? Well, the drone can be yours. All you have to do is get along with Mary for one month, just four short weeks, and that drone will be yours."

Josh then has the most loving, altruistic, patient, and kind four weeks he has ever had with Mary. Josh's mom and dad are amazed that for a whole month Mary hasn't cried once. They are basking in their parental wisdom and success. So Josh's dad orders the drone and even pays for a rush delivery. The drone arrives, and Josh and his dad assemble it together. They give it a little test drive in the backyard and fifteen minutes later, they hear Mary crying as Josh is chasing her around the back yard with his little drone.

Now think with me about what has happened here. The promise

and purchase of the drone were Josh's parents' attempt to produce something that they have no ability to produce. What looked like a stunning success was a massive failure. You see, Josh wasn't nice to his sister for those four weeks because he had come to the point where he saw how wrong his mistreatment of her was, confessed it to God and his sister, and prayed for help to be more loving toward her. Not at all! There was no recognition of wrong and desire for change at all inside Josh. He hadn't begun to feel a new compassion and love for Mary. In fact, the only reason Josh was nice to Mary for four weeks is because Josh loves Josh! This self-love was the same reason he mistreated her in the first place. Now, not only has the self-love, which caused Josh to do what was fun for him but hurtful to his sister, remained, but it's been rewarded. And what Josh does with the new drone proves that there has been no change in him at all. This will sound harsh, but it needs to be said: Josh's parents' strategy is neither Christian nor parenting because they are not functioning as ambassadors of what God wants to do in Josh's life and because they are not accepting their inability. They are not functioning as tools of change in God's hands.

But there is more. Although I'm sure Josh's parents are not consciously intending to do this, they are teaching Josh a skill they probably don't want him to have. It's the skill of moral economics. As the parental rewards are waved before him, Josh will do a cost/benefit analysis. He will ask himself, "Is the reward they are offering me a big enough payment for the behavior they want from me?" Josh will learn to negotiate with his parents and up the ante. If a child is negotiating reward with his parents, he has no moral guilt and desire to do what is right inside him. He is just after what he wants, and if a little temporary obedience is the price he has to pay, he's willing.

Change is about learning what is right, acknowledging that it is right, confessing that you have been wrong, committing to a new way of living, and seeking the help you need to do it. None of these things have happened inside Josh, because his parents sadly succumbed to the temptation to opt for control rather than to give themselves to the hard, exhausting, and often discouraging work of being tools of change in the hands of the only One who can produce it. It is tempting for every parent, on any given day, in one of those hard moments to see momentary control as better than long-term change and to reach for whatever tool is at your fingertips to get your kid to do what you want him to do.

Like fear, this tool will produce what you're looking for only for a while. When your child is young, there are many small and inexpensive things that she might want which would grant you momentary control. But as she matures, the cost for what would produce what you want from her goes up, until there is nothing that you can afford that might motivate her to do what you want. It's at this point that many grieved parents say, "What has happened to my child?" The answer is, nothing has happened to your child; this is who she has always been. You have just masked what was really going on inside her with an endless series of rewards.

Shame

Shame and guilt are power tools that parents use more frequently than we recognize. "I can't believe that you would even think of doing such a thing!" "When I was your age, I would have never thought of doing that!" "In all my parenting days, I never thought that I'd have to deal with such a thing!" "After all I've done for you, and this is the way you're going to treat me." "I sometimes wonder where in the world you came from." "You have no idea what you've put us through." None of these statements are about wooing and winning your child for what is right. None of these statements are meant to help them assess their hearts, confess their wrongs, and reach out for help. These statements are about parents reaching for a power tool: guilt. Whether it's intentional or not, saying these things is an attempt to shame our children into what is right.

Making your child feel horizontal guilt (this guilt is about you) is very different from giving your child insight into his heart that causes him to feel vertical guilt (this is guilt with respect to God) and the desire to change. For example, a mother says to her children, who are driving her and her husband crazy, "I remember when your father was a happy man. It was before we had children. Now, he is so distressed by the things you do that he can barely concentrate at work. Yesterday he called home eighteen times because he was so concerned and distracted, and if he can't concentrate at work, then he could lose his job, and if he loses his job, then what will happen to us? Look at him walking up the driveway. You can see how much he dreads opening the door and hearing about the horrible things you've done to one another all day!" I've set this up humorously, but you get the point.

In these moments as parents we are not working to help our children see what they need to see so that they would become dissatisfied with who they are and reach out for our help and the Lord's. In these moments, we are denying our powerlessness and reaching for whatever tool is at our disposal that will help us to control our kids. Guilt and shame are very powerful tools, because it's natural for our children to want us to accept and appreciate them. It's natural for them to want us to be pleased and proud of them. Every child ever born wants to be loved. So guilt and shame are temporarily effective tools of parental control.

Notice that I said "temporarily effective." Like all tools of parental control, guilt and shame have a short-term positive harvest and a long-term negative legacy. At some point every child quits being moved by guilt and begins to get tired of being put down. At some point children begin to understand the dynamics of their relationship with you. At some point, even though they cannot verbalize it, children begin to understand the difference between control and patient love. They begin to see the difference between you using old tools to get them to *do* something and you lovingly being God's tool to help them *be* something. At some point they begin to distance themselves from you in order to protect themselves from the guilt and shame that often seems to come when you are near.

The lack of communication, closeness, and affection that exists between parents and their older children is often the sad legacy of the ways we tried to control our kids. Our heavenly Father is never content with just controlling us. Control is no problem for him; he's sovereign after all. But in grace he wanted more for us. So he devised a plan that would result in our forgiveness and complete transformation. In Jesus he made a way for us to see our sin, to confess it, to be granted complete forgiveness, and to be blessed with both the desire and the power to change. He is the Redeemer, and so he is unwilling to settle for anything less than radical personal heart and life change. It is important to understand two things:

1. This is the work that he has called us to as parents, and we cannot settle for anything less.
2. We have no ability to do this work on our own, and recognizing our inability is essential to being what we are supposed to be and doing what we are supposed to do as parents.

Here's the good news: we can admit our powerlessness as parents and not live in constant panic and frustration. We can embrace our inability and not worry our way through our parenting years. Why? Because as parents we serve a gloriously loving and powerful Redeemer. He loves our children infinitely more than we do and as evidence of that love, he has placed them in a family of faith where the story of his love will be heard again and again. He has power beyond our ability to understand. The same mind-boggling power he exercised to raise Jesus from the dead, he now unleashes to give sight, conviction, power, and desire to our desperately needy children. In grace he will never turn his back on your cries as a parent and on your children's cries as they reach out for him. He delights in love. He delights in reconciliation. He delights in repentance and change. He delights in showering his power down on his children to do for them what is his will, but what they cannot do for themselves.

Good parenting lives at the intersection of a humble admission of personal powerlessness and a confident rest in the power and grace of God. The questions for you right here, right now are: Do you have that rest? Is your parenting driven by worry that causes you to do and say things that you shouldn't do or say? Do you find yourself being willing to settle for control, rather than giving yourself to the hard process of change? Are you working to get your children to do what you want them to do rather than helping them to be what God wants them to be? Do you parent with a powerful and loving Redeemer in view?

God is with you. He wants what is best for you and your children, and no one but he has the power to produce it. He has not placed the burden of change on your shoulders because he would not require you to do what you cannot do. God has simply called you as a parent to be a humble and faithful tool of change in the lives of your children. And for that there is moment by moment by moment grace.

5

Identity

Principle: If you are not resting as a parent in your identity in Christ, you will look for identity in your children.

FEW PARENTS THINK ABOUT IT and almost none are aware that they do it every single day. Your parenting is always shaped by where you look for identity. This may seem like the most impractical suggestion you've ever read in a parenting book, but what this chapter is about explains much of the struggle we all experience as we seek to parent our children. It explains why our children have a profound ability to hurt us. It defines why they can make us so angry. It helps you understand how your children have the ability to steal your joy and rob you of your sleep. It explains why you take the success or failure of your children so personally. It defines why your children have the ability to make you feel hugely proud or deeply embarrassed. No matter how much you love your children, the things I have just described are not love struggles; they are identity struggles, and when you get a hold of this, it will change how you see yourself as a parent and how you daily interact with your children.

Sally put her whole life on hold for one purpose and one purpose alone: to make something of her children. She read long books to them before they could talk and had them in music school when kindergarten was still a few years off. Once her children were in school, she not only demanded academic excellence for them, but she chose a variety of extracurricular activities that they were required to participate in, because she thought they would prepare her children for a successful future. Between school and all the other required involvements, Sally's children had almost no time to themselves. Even the weekends were filled with trips to the museum, the symphony's matinee performances, and community service projects. Sally was committed to her dream of lavishly successful children, so not only was she driven and unrelenting, but she drove them too.

I met Sally's son, Jamie, because Sally reached out to me for help with him. His grades at school began to fall, and he had missed showing up for some of his regularly scheduled responsibilities. Sally had begun to worry, but it all came to a head one morning when Jamie refused to leave his room, refused to go to school, and said he had no plans to ever touch his violin again. This kicked off an ugly two-hour battle between Jamie and Sally. Finally, he went to school, but when she went to pick him up for his music lesson, he was nowhere to be found and didn't show up at home until ten o'clock that night.

Sally saw the dream that she had worked for all those years slipping through her fingers, and she was in a panic. She called me and said that Jamie was out of control, that he would not talk to her, and that she needed help fast. Two days later I met with Sally and Jamie for the first time. I want to describe to you what the two people looked like who sat in front of me that day. Sally was clearly angry and impatient; she fidgeted and sighed. Jamie looked like a beaten and defeated young man; he sat with his head down as if he were facing his execution. I tried my best to interview Sally as to what was going on, but she resisted and told me that she didn't know why I was wasting time talking to her and that it was Jamie who needed the help. She said more than once, "I have worked too hard for too long to throw it all away because my son woke up one morning and decided he wanted to be lazy. I need you to help me get the old Jamie back."

So I asked Sally to leave for a few minutes so I could talk to Jamie alone. She wasn't happy leaving, but she did. The first question I asked Jamie when we were alone together was what was going on. I wanted it to be open-ended. I didn't want him to think I was his mother's hired gun, although my heart went out to her. As soon as the question had come out of my mouth, Jamie began to cry. He was embarrassed that he was crying, but I assured him it was okay. Quietly, but with the fatalistic anger of a broken young man, he said, "I can't do it anymore, I just can't. It's never enough. The pressure never stops. I have no free time, I have no friends, I have no choices, all I have is work from the moment I get up in the morning until I crash in bed. I practice two hours before school, I have writing classes, music lessons, and college prep after school, and then homework and two more hours of practicing before I hit the bed. And, oh, I forgot, I am required to participate in at least one sport each quarter. I'm not Superman. I just can't do it anymore, so I told my mom that I quit, I wouldn't do it anymore. I haven't been to school and all my other stuff for a few days because I have refused to get out of bed and when I finally get out of bed, I won't leave my room. If I had some place to run to, I would run, but I don't."

As I listened to Jamie, I knew this wasn't a ploy. He wasn't just messing with his mom. I knew Jamie meant what he was saying. He had gotten off the success train, and there was nothing that would get him back on again. But there was something else I knew. I knew that I needed to talk to his mom because I knew this mess wasn't just about Jamie being rebellious and lazy. It was about her too, about heart issues for her that were deep and would be hard for her to accept.

Ask yourself: "What is going on when a parent drives a child to mental, physical, and emotional exhaustion, to the point where the child is willing to throw his or her life away to escape the demands? What is going on inside parents when they are with their child every day, yet they don't see that something is wrong, they don't notice the breakdown as it's happening? What is going on when the child is not allowed to stop because the parent can't face what it will mean if the child stops? What is going on in the heart of a parent who is more focused on success than on the child who is required to deliver it?"

I invited Sally back in and told her how concerned I was for Jamie, and then I told her that I would like to counsel not only Jamie, but her as well. As I said it, I could see her posture stiffen. "I didn't come here for counsel. I think I'm doing quite well, given the burdens of parenting I'm bearing." I tried to kindly tell her that I didn't think it would work to talk to Jamie without talking to her as well. She could hear only that I was taking Jamie's part, and she told me that I wouldn't be talking to either her or Jamie. Obviously offended, she left quickly.

I wish I could tell you that Sally and Jamie's story is unique, but it's not. I think there are thousands and thousands of parents who are doing what Sally did with Jamie. It's not because they're unkind, unloving, or abusive. It's not because they don't care what happens to their children. I am about to say something that will confuse you. I'm convinced this success-driven system of unrelenting rules, performances, and obligations exists because these parents care too much about the present and future success of their children. The desire for successful children is a good thing that has become a bad thing because it's become a ruling thing. It causes parents to do things that ultimately crush and embitter their children, all in the name of something good. Read on and let me clear up any confusion.

The Identity Quest

Human beings were designed to be interpreters. We were created to be rational. We were made to be always thinking. Our thoughts always precede and therefore shape and direct our activity. No action that we take, no choice that we make, and none of the words that we say are in a vacuum. All our actions and reactions are connected to who we think we are, who we think God is, what we think life is about, what we think is important, where we go to find help, and what we look to in order to give us peace, rest, and security. At street level, we don't really live based on the facts of our existence, but based on the sense that we are making out of those facts. That's why you can have two people in the very same situation who respond in very different ways to the same set of facts. Your belief system or your worldview is always being exposed by how you parent those who have been entrusted to your care. You don't respond as a parent because of who your children are and because of what they're doing, but because of the way you make sense out of who they are and what you're doing.

Here are a couple examples. If you say to your child, "I can't believe you would do this to me!" you are not responding to the facts of the situation, but to your interpretation of those facts. Your interpretation is that what your child has done, whether he acknowledges it or not, is a personal attack on you in some way. Or if you spend more time punishing your children for breaking the law than you do talking to your children about Jesus, who perfectly kept the law on their behalf because God knew they never would, your response is not shaped by the fact of their disobedience, but by the sense you are making of their disobedience and how it will change. It is important for all parents to examine the system of belief that shapes their moment-by-moment interactions with their children.

One of the central components of this personal system of belief is the question of identity and meaning and purpose. Every parent asks and in some way answers the "Who am I?" question, and every parent asks and answers the "Where is my meaning and purpose in life to be found?" question. And the way that you answer these questions will determine how you speak and act toward your kids. There are only two places for you and me to look for identity. One place to look is vertically, getting our identity and the direction and assessment of potential from God—from his love and acceptance, his forgiving grace, his constant presence, his power and his promises, and the glory of all of these that he's showered down on us. When we do this, we come to parenting with hearts that are full and satisfied, we live with courage and hope, and we are not needy, because we have found all that we need in him. As Peter writes, "His divine power has granted to us all things that pertain to life and godliness, through the knowledge of him who called us to his own glory and excellence, by which he has granted to us his precious and very great promises, so that through them you may become partakers of the divine nature, having escaped from the corruption that is in the world because of sinful desire" (2 Pet. 1:3–4).

Notice the period of time that the hope of this passage is addressing. Peter is not talking about salvation past or salvation future, but about the work of God for you right here, right now. As a Christian parent, no matter what is happening with your kids, you can wake up in the morning and know that you are deeply and faithfully loved by the most important person in the universe. Because God loves you, he hasn't left you to your own wisdom, strength, and resources. Because he loves you, he will never forsake you in your parenting struggle. Because he loves you, he has connected you to things that are vastly bigger than you. Because he loves you, he not only forgives you, but he also gives you the grace to do better. Because he loves you, he works daily to grow and change you so that you are better able to do what he's called you to do. Because he loves you, he works to satisfy your heart and fill you with joy that doesn't depend on circumstances. He loves you so much that he has come to live inside you. He doesn't just make promises to you; he is present with you in all his power, grace, and glory so that you can have peace of heart, purpose and direction, and courage to face your parenting day.

If you are not resting in your vertical identity, you will look horizontally, searching to find yourself and your reason for living in something in the creation. That could be your possessions, your accomplishments, your career, your spouse, your children, and the list goes on. The problem with this is that created things were never designed to give you identity. They were never designed to satisfy your heart and give you peace. They were not made to give you meaning and purpose. Every good thing in creation is designed to point you to the One who alone is able to give you the identity, peace, and meaning that your heart seeks.

It never works to look to a broken, dysfunctional creation for identity. It always leads to disappointment, fear, anxiety, drivenness, and more control than any one of us will ever have (read 2 Pet. 1:8–9). Peter actually proposes that you can be a Christian and have a life that is "ineffective or unfruitful" because you have forgotten who you are and what you have been given. Sadly, I think this describes many parents. They are looking to get from their children what they have already been given in Christ, and they don't know that they are doing it. And their anxiety and drivenness as a parent is the result of *identity amnesia*. Identity amnesia will always lead to identity replacement. What this means for a parent is that if you are not getting your identity from God and the work of his Son, you will probably try to get it from your children.

Now there are three things to say about trying to get your identity from your children. First, it is a very natural thing to do and a very hard thing to fight. In fact, probably every parent falls into this trap in some way. Second, parenting is a miserable place to look for identity. Think about it: you are parenting lost, rebellious, foolish, blind, self-ruling sinners. I'm not picking on your children. I have just described every fallen human being born into God's world. Third, it is a crushing burden for your children to have to get up every morning and carry the heavy load of your identity and meaning and purpose and all the expectations and demands that flow from it. No child will carry that load well.

What I have just described is exactly what was happening to Sally and Jamie, and neither one of them knew it. Sally thought she was just being a good mom. But what she didn't realize is that that system of unrelenting demands was not being done by Sally for Jamie, but by Sally for Sally. Don't get me wrong. I don't think Sally was self-centered, "it's all about me," but she was looking for Jamie to give her a kind of meaning, purpose, and peace of heart that he could never give her. She looked to this fifteen-year-old boy to give her life worth, and he was breaking under the load. The result was that they were both miserable and in a war that neither of them understood or wanted to be in.

Don't be too hard on Sally. In some way we all look for identity and security where it cannot be found. We all tend to try to get too much of our meaning and purpose from our children. We all tend to ride the up-and-down roller coaster of their compliance or resistance. We all tend to need them to be successful too much. And when we look to our children to give us what we already have in Jesus, we drive them to succeed not simply because we know it is best for them, but because we need their success to feel good about ourselves and to have a reason to get up in the morning and continue. We need their love and respect in order to feel good about our lives. We need them to look a certain way and act a certain way in order to feel that our work as a parent has been worth it. So although we love our kids, we don't just bring love to our parenting of them, but neediness, which brings self-centeredness, an entitlement, a demandingness, and a drivenness to our parenting. Even though we don't know it, we begin to treat our kids as if they were given to us to be a living argument or case statement for the fact that we are good people and are doing our job in life well. And perhaps the desire to raise children that we can be proud of is really a desire to feel good about ourselves and the way we have lived our life.

Parents, this is an exhausting and discouraging way to live. It is exhausting to need little, immature sinners to perform well in order to feel good about yourself and your life. It's exhausting to chase success after success, never being fully satisfied. It's discouraging to feed off the love of someone too immature to give it to you faithfully. It's discouraging to personalize your children's failures as if they were intentionally plotting against you. It's exhausting to load your schedule with activity after activity until you have little free time left because you need your children to succeed. It's discouraging to have to face the sin and struggle of your children when you need near perfection to feel it's been worth it. It's exhausting and discouraging to ask your kids to give you what they cannot give and for you to need so deeply what you have no power to produce. And as your children get older, they begin to realize that much of what you have been doing has not been for them, but for yourself.

Parents, your children can't give you life. They can't give you sturdy hope. They can't give you worth. They can't give you peace of heart. They can't give you right desires and motivation. They can't give you strength to go on. They can't give you confidence and courage in the middle of a trial. And they can't give you that ultimate, heart-satisfying love that you long for. I'm going to say it in a way that I hope will get your attention. It just never works to ask your children to be your own personal saviors. This is a burden they will never bear well, and it will introduce trouble and struggle into your relationship with them. Jesus is your life, and this frees you and your children from the burden of asking them to give you what your Savior has already given you.

Sally was growingly fearful, angry, and discouraged, and Jamie was exhausted and angry too. The more she demanded, the more he resisted. Her relationship with Jamie was disintegrating right before her eyes, but she did not see it and kept driving forward. It was all the sad result of looking to get her identity from a broken and immature young man who would never be able to deliver it to her. Parents, we can do better because of the presence, promises, and power of Jesus that have been lavished on us by grace.

So How Do You Know?

How do you know if you're putting your identity on the shoulders of your children? How can you know if you are asking your kids to do for you what God has already done for you in his Son? What are the signs that your parenting is driven more by what you need from your children than by what God wants to do through you in your children? Here are five sure indications.

1. Too much focus on success. Of course, if you love your children, you are going to want them to do well. No parent wants her children to fail. You want your children to achieve and to be respected. All parents want their children to try harder and to accomplish more. But this is very different from becoming too focused, too obsessed, and too driven by the achievements of your children.

Could it be that you want your children to succeed too much because you *need* them to succeed? Could it be that your children are beginning to break under the heavy load of your expectations? Could it be that the resistance you are getting from your children is there not because they are rebellious and lazy, but because you are asking too much of them? Could it be that you are so focused on your children's accomplishments that you have not paid enough attention to the condition of their hearts? Could it be that your focus on success as a parent is not spiritually healthy for you or your children because this focus is rooted in asking your children to give you that satisfaction of heart that they will never be able to give?

2. Too much concern about reputation. This cannot be repeated enough. Write down what you're about to read and tape it to the mirror you look at as you begin each day: *God didn't give you your children to build your reputation but to publicly proclaim his.* Vertical identity amnesia leaves us all too worried about what others think about us and what we are doing. It produces in many parents a fear of man that causes us to hide and deny our struggles and present to the world children who are more perfect than any of our children actually are. And when you are too concerned about your public face as a parent, you don't seek the help you need in your struggle because in order to seek that help you have to admit that you're not doing so well. It never works to treat a child, who is still broken and needs to be daily rescued by grace, as your trophy.

Could it be that your reputation as a parent means too much to you? Could it be that what others think of your children is too important to you? Could it be that you're asking immature little sinners to go out and polish your reputation as a mom or dad? Could it be that your desire for reputation keeps you from admitting and seeking help for those places where your parenting is broken?

3. Too great a desire for control. If you need your children to succeed and enhance your reputation because, as a parent, you need the identity that comes from that, then you are going to want to control situations, locations, and people to make sure that happens. There is a significant difference between exercising proper parental authority over your children and a desire to exercise such control over their lives that you can be sure to get from them what you think you need. Under this system of control, children never have the freedom to make mistakes, to learn how to evaluate choices, to decide between options, to develop a reasonable schedule, to assess their potential, to recognize gifts, to discern when they are overcommitted, to learn how to leave time for a healthy relationship with God and others, and to see how good things become bad things when they become ruling things.

Could it be that your desire for success has caused you to exercise a level of control that actually is in the way of your child's growth and development? Could it be that your anxiety as a parent comes from the fact that you are trying to exercise control over things you don't have the power to control? Could it be that your quest for parenting control has kept you from resting in the perfectly wise control of your heavenly Father over you and your children?

4. Too much emphasis on doing *rather than* being. In our parental struggle with success, reputation, and control, we begin to lose sight of what is actually of greatest value to the One we represent. Think about this: God really did harness all the forces of the natural world and direct all the various events of human history so that his

Son would come, and by his life and death, rescue us from us. God did this radical, life-altering thing not first so that your children would be successful, but so that they would be united again in a love relationship with him and live lives that are pleasing in his sight. What you and your children need most is not success; it's redemption. What you and your children need is not the glory of personal achievement but rescue from your bondage to self-glory so that you can enjoy the freedom of living for the glory of another.

Could it be that the achievements that you want your children to produce have kept you from focusing on the things that they desperately need but cannot produce? Could it be that the focus on physical, social, and educational accomplishments has kept you from focusing on their hearts? Could it be that your focus on what you want them to do has put you in the way of what God alone can form your children to be? Could it be that what God values in your children is different from the values that drive your expectations of and responses to your children?

5. Too much temptation to make it personal. When you need your children to be successful, when you need them to build your reputation, and when you need to be in control, you will personalize what is not personal. In subtle ways the focus shifts from how their behavior is viewed by God to how it affects you. It becomes "how could you do this to me?" rather than "this violates what God has called you to be." It simply devastates a relationship to make something personal that is not personal. It makes your children feel that they are being accused of something they did not do. Let's say your son leaves a royal mess in the kitchen, and you say to him, "After all I do for you, and this is the way you leave the kitchen?" Now, examine the logic there. Is what he did personal or simply the result of the laziness and self-centeredness of sin that we all still carry around with us? Do you really think that that morning he woke up and said to himself, "At 7:12 a.m. I'm going to drive my mom crazy. I know what I will do; I'll leave a big mess all over the kitchen. Yeah, that will drive her crazy." Of course, that is not what happened! What he did was not personal in that way, and neither are many of the other things he does that you have to deal with as his parent. To personalize it misses the point of how God is using that moment to reveal his heart to you, and it causes you to accuse him of intentions that he didn't actually have.

Could it be that tension has been caused in your relationship to your children because you have tended to personalize what is not personal? Could it be that your desire to get things from your children has caused you to take personal offense at things that are not personal? Could it be that in important parenting moments your tendency to take offense causes you to stand against your children rather than to stand with them in their struggle with sin? Could it be that taking personal offense has caused you to respond with anger to what God is calling you to meet with grace?

Isn't it good to know that God's presence with us and provision for us are so full, faithful, and complete that we really do come to our parental calling with everything we need to be what he's called us to be and to do what he's called us to do? Isn't it good to know that because Jesus gives us life overflowing, we are freed from looking for life from our children or anywhere else? Isn't it good to know that because we are the children of God, we have reason to continue even on our worst, most disastrous parenting day? Isn't it good to know that as Jesus fully satisfies our hearts, we don't have to ask our children to provide that satisfaction? It really is the completeness of the work of Jesus for us that frees us from coming to our parenting task needy, exhausted, and discouraged, asking our children to give us what they will never ever be able to give. The question of the moment is, Are you experiencing that wonderful freedom as a parent?

6

process

Principle: You must be committed as a parent to long-view parenting because change is a process and not an event.

WE ALL WANT IT and none of us ever get it. It can be so frustrating at times. You would love to have it just once, but it seems to evade you every time. As a parent, you probably don't consciously think about it much, but the desire is there, and it stimulates much impatience and disappointment. We all tend to think that we have the power to produce it, but we don't. We all say and do things that we think will create it, but our words and actions simply don't have the power that we think they do. Here's what I'm talking about. We want parenting to be a series of events rather than a lifelong process. So in moments of discipline we get loaded for bear; we get cranked up emotionally and think that if we are stern enough and loud enough, and make threats that are big enough, we will win, and our children will instantly change. I have had parent after parent say something like this to me: "Paul, I've tried everything you have suggested and it hasn't worked." My question at that point always is, "How do you know?"

Let me give you a couple examples. Your four-year-old son just hit his two-year-old sister. You say, "Why would you do such a thing?" Now what you want him to say is, "I hit her because of the sin in my heart. It makes me selfish, jealous, and violent, and I am a person who needs to be rescued from myself. You know, Mom, the greatest danger to me lives inside me not outside me, and for that I need a Savior." He's hit her seventy times before, you've had this conversation before, and you're tired of having it. You just want him to confess and seek help for once. Couldn't it all happen in just one conversation? Instead, what he answers to your question is, "She always takes my stuff. I tell her not to, but she won't listen. Why don't you yell at her for not listening?" At that point you're very discouraged, and you can feel yourself losing it.

Or it's 12:25 a.m. and the teenager, whom you told to be in before midnight and who promised she would, is not home yet, and although she has a cell phone, has not called. You're sitting in the living room, staring at the front door, cell phone in your hand, and steaming. Suddenly, you hear the car pull into the driveway, screech to a halt, and in seconds the door burst open. You've been in this scene with her several times. She's told you she hates her curfew, but that she'll try to do better. She always acts irritated when you remind her once again when she is supposed to be in. You don't want to hear her catalog of quasi-creative excuses, and you don't want her to tell you again that a few minutes late doesn't make any difference or that at least she's not drinking or taking drugs. The conversation you wanted to have, where she would acknowledge her irresponsibility, quit shifting the blame, and own her need of help, is once again not going to happen, so you tell her to go to bed and you'll talk about it in the morning. You go to bed discouraged that you have to go through these scenes again and again.

Here the gospel of Jesus Christ provides the ultimate model of what God has called us to as parents. Think about how God the Father works change into our lives as his children. Because of the complete work of Jesus, we are welcomed into God's family, with all of the rights and privileges of being his children. We have been fully justified and completely accepted, but we are not complete, because there is massive change that needs to take place in us. Let me say it this way: the power of sin has been broken, but the presence of sin still remains and will be progressively eradicated. The most important word in the last sentence is *progressively*. Here's what is important to understand: the Father's work of justification is an event, but his work of transformation is literally a life-long process. When justifying you, God is fully aware that he is committing himself to a day-by-day process of illumining, confronting, convicting, forgiving, transforming, and delivering grace.

I love how Paul characterizes this process in 1 Timothy 1:16: "But I received mercy for this reason, that in me, as the foremost, Jesus Christ might display his perfect patience as an example to those who were to believe in him for eternal life." Paul is saying, "Because I am the worst of all sinners, Jesus will be able to use me as a case study of how patient he is able and willing to be as he does his work of grace. So those who need to entrust themselves to the Father will be encouraged by the extent of his patience."

Parents, there is your model. Parenting is not a series of dramatic confrontation-confession events, but rather a life-long process of incremental awareness and progressive change. The four-year-old will not say after you confront him, "I am a self-centered, self-ruling idolater in need of redemption." The middle schooler will not become a fully transformed human being and the teenager will still need your parenting wisdom. I think that the desire for overnight change gets us into trouble.

It's the day you're leaving for vacation, and you have parented your children all year long. It would be nice if they could give you a break during your vacation. Now, consider what you're wishing for. You're hoping that the little sinners, who needed so much of your attention the day before, have been transformed during the night into fully sanctified, self-parenting little human beings. But you're not seven-tenths of a mile down the road, and they're already fighting in the back of the van. You begin to lose it and threaten to turn around, drive back home, and cancel the vacation.

A misunderstanding of what you've been called to as a parent will always set up unrealistic expectations of your children and frustrations as a parent that will tempt you to do and say things that you shouldn't do or say. Let me explain.

The Blind Leading the Blind

Parenting would be infinitely easier if all you were dealing with was wrong behavior. But what you're dealing with is something deeper and more deadly. The Bible states very clearly that one of the most dangerous aspects of sin, which all parents deal with personally and which all parents deal with in their children, is the fact that sin blinds (see Isa. 6:10; 43:8, 18; Zeph. 1:17; Matt. 15:14; John 2:10; 2 Cor. 4:4; Heb. 3:12–13). I have said it many times: "Sin blinds, and guess who it blinds first? I have no problem seeing the sin of my family members, neighbors, and friends, but I can be quite surprised when somehow my sin is exposed." This is what you are dealing with in your children.

It would be bad enough that children are predisposed by sin to rebel against authority, to want to write their own rules, and to therefore do what is wrong. But as you're dealing with these things, you're also parenting a little person who does not see his sin or himself accurately. What is wrong doesn't look so wrong to them, and who they are isn't apparent to them. Your children are not just selfish and rebellious; they are blind. What, by God's grace, is clear to you is not clear to them. What seems obvious to you is not obvious to them. And the response that we think should be natural is counterintuitive to them. They think they are okay, but they're not okay. They think they are right, but they're not right. They think they have decided wisely, but they have been foolish. And because they think these things, they don't think that they need your parental help. No wonder our children are resistant!

The problem with the four-year-old is not just that he hit his sister, but that he feels fully justified in hitting her. He thinks she is to blame, and he thinks that she needs your correction more than he does. And he thinks these things because he is blind. Your teenage daughter doesn't think that repeatedly coming in late is a big deal. She does think you're being overly dramatic and judgmental. She does think she is a responsible person, with valid excuses. She does think that you just need to chill because she doesn't really have a problem that requires your attention. And she thinks these things because she is blind.

No parent is able to escape the deceiving power of sin. All parents need to understand the power of spiritual blindness as they think of the task that God has called them to. Your job would be so much easier if you were parenting a spiritually sighted person, who saw herself accurately. But there is more.

Spiritual blindness is unlike physical blindness in one very significant way. When you are physically blind, you know you are blind and you immediately do things to compensate for this significant physical deficiency. I have a friend who has been blind since he was nine years old. I am amazed by the many things he has learned to do, and do well, that we would think require sight. Because he was confronted with his blindness as a child, he has been on a life-long quest to limit the restrictions blindness places on his life. When I am with him, he never fails to amaze me as I experience again the creative way he works around his blindness. It may seem silly to say, but all of this creativity has been fueled by the fact that he knows he is blind.

Personal spiritual blindness, the kind of blindness that is in every child of every parent, is not like what my friend is dealing with. Why? Because spiritual blindness carries with it one component that makes it all the more dangerous and hard to deal with. Unlike physical blindness, where you know you are blind, spiritually blind people are blind to their blindness. They are blind, but they think they see quite well. Spiritual blindness happens at the intersection of the deceptiveness of sin and the delusion of self-knowledge. Both of these are operating in the hearts of all of our children. They are not just misbehaving; they are blind to their misbehavior and the sin of their hearts that creates it. Understanding this alters the way we need to think about the parenting process.

The conversation with the four-year-old is complicated by the fact that you're not talking to a sighted person. The confrontation with the teenage girl is made much more difficult by the fact that you are talking to someone who is blind. It's not that your children don't confess quickly and change quickly—it's that they don't see what you see. And because they don't see what you see, they think you are wrong and needlessly judgmental. You're just not going to get one-conversation turnarounds, and going into times of correction with those expectations will create lots of irritation, impatience, and discouragement inside you.

But something else needs to be factored into this discussion. When it comes to spiritual blindness, you and I are more like our children than unlike them. Sin renders us blind too. Sin makes us all too self-assured and self-reliant too. Sin causes us to see ourselves as okay when we're not okay. Sin causes us to resist correction and to be offended and defensive when we are confronted. Sin makes us activate our inner lawyers and rush to our defense when it would be better for us to listen, consider, and be willing to confess. Like our children, we are in need of a Father who will patiently work over a long period of time to help us to see. We need a Father who, in mercy, will not demand instantaneous change. We need a Father who understands our condition and confronts us not just with his rebuke, but with his grace. And although you are an adult and have perhaps known God for years, you still have pockets of spiritual blindness in you and you still tend to resist the care that you yet need. Like our children, you and I do the same wrong things over and over again because we are not only blind, but we are blind to our blindness. We need compassionate, patient care if we are ever going to change, and so do our children.

Parenting, the Never-Ending Conversation

So how should all of this restructure and reshape the way we think about the task that God has called us to as parents? What should our expectations and commitments be? And what character is required so that we can be part of what God is seeking to do in the lives of our children and not in the way of it? What needs to be done, we can't do, but we have been chosen to be a ready tool in the hands of the One who is ready and able to do it. So, if you want to be a sharp and ready tool in the hands of the great Author of change, here are three mentalities that need to shape your parenting.

1. You Need to Parent with a Process Mentality

It's important to make the mental/spiritual shift from viewing parenting as a series of unrelated corrective encounters to viewing parenting as a life-long connected process. Since change is most often a process and seldom an event, you have to remember that you can't look for a dramatic transformational conclusion to your encounters with your children. Seldom is change the result of a dramatic moment. So you have partial conversations and unfinished moments, but in each moment you are imparting wisdom to your child, each moment you are exposing your child's heart, each moment you are building your child's self-awareness, each moment you are enlivening your child's conscience, each moment you are giving your child great God-awareness, each moment you are constructing a biblical worldview for your child, and each moment you are giving the Spirit of God an opportunity to do things in and for your child that you cannot do.

The wise Father of you and your children designed parenting to be a bit-by-bit, piece-by-piece process. He has called you to take advantage of the little moments of life to take little steps with your children. He has called you to be content with adding another piece to their view of themselves, God, others, and life. He has called you to be content with adding another piece to their moral/spiritual awareness. Here's what parenting is: it's unfinished people (we parents) being used of God as agents of transformation in the lives of unfinished people. And, yes, it is true that like you, your children will leave your home still unfinished. One of the last things Jesus said to his disciples is that he had many more things to teach them, but they were not at that time able to bear them. So he promised them that he would send another teacher to complete his work. The world's best teacher had a process mentality and because he did, he was willing to leave his work to unfinished people (see John 16:12–15).

2. You Need to See Parenting as One Unending Conversation

As a parent, I find this mentality incredibly freeing. Let me explain. You are freed from the pressure of needing to get from your child what you are never going to get in a single conversation. You know that this conversation is only one moment in an ongoing conversation that began when the child was born and will probably not even end when your child leaves your home. You are liberated from having to load your hopes for your child into one conversation, because you know that you live with this child and you will get many more opportunities.

You see, God loves your child even more than you do, and because he loves her, he has put her in a family of faith, and he will expose what is wrong with that child again and again so that you have opportunity after opportunity to take yet another step in the process of awareness, conviction, commitment, and change that he has called you to be part of in the life of your child. So each day you look for another opportunity to advance that critical conversation one more step and because you do, you don't consider those moments where correction is needed to be interruptions or hassles, but gifts of grace afforded you by a God who is at work in the hearts and lives of your children. So you're not mad at your children for needing you; you're happy for another opportunity to continue the process. Here, in a phrase, is what you are committing yourself to: *many mini-moments of change.*

It may be a few moments at bedtime; it may be a brief talk at the dinner table; it may be a few carefully chosen words at the mall; it may be a few comments after school; it may be a back-and-forth discussion in the SUV. But you're called to be thankful for each one and for the incremental steps that are being taken to rescue, restore, and transform your children. You get up each day aware of what will be required, but thankful that for another day you can take more steps with your children in the most important process in the world.

3. You Need to Parent with a Project Mentality

Instead of being reactive as a parent, you must live with your children with a sense of project. What does that mean? You know your children; you know where they tend to be weak, blind, tempted, and rebellious, and where they struggle. So you look for opportunities to address what God has shown you about the needy heart of each individual child. What this means is that every day you look to engage your child with consideration of what you already know is important. You point out simple little things to the four-year-old and much more sophisticated things to the teenager, but in each instance you move the conversation along because you are parenting with a sense of project. And because you are, you are ready to capture another God-given opportunity.

Because most of us don't parent with a sense of project, prepared for when God will give us the next opportunity, our parenting tends to be reactive. Surprised that another problem has called us into action, we react to the moment in the best way we can. The problem with this is that reactive parenting tends to be *emotionally* reactive. Because we are not carrying around with us this project mentality, we tend to see these moments as interruptions and hassles, and because we do, we tend to deal with them emotionally. What this creates for your child is an irregular and inconsistent authority structure. Yesterday, you weren't doing well emotionally so the racket in the house drove you nuts and you yelled at your kids. Today, you are feeling good and the same noise level that got them in trouble yesterday doesn't get them in trouble today.

Sadly, rather than growing in a sense of need for and submission to the authority that God has placed in their lives, many children become *emotional weathermen*. They have come to understand that the rules of the house tend to change with the emotion of the parent who is present. So they're constantly checking the weather in order to gauge what they can get away with and what they can't. Because parental engagement and authority have been inconsistent, their submission to it is inconsistent as well. The conversational process is not being advanced, the children are not growing, and the parents are not the tools of change that God has appointed them to be. We can do better.

Following the Father

If you want to be part of the Father's process in the lives of your children, you have to commit yourself to being part of doing it his way. Let me say it this way: if you are going to be a tool in the hands of the Father, you need not only to submit to his work, but also to commit to his character. Now, permit me to be honest. What gets in the way of good parenting is not a lack of opportunity. What gets in the way of good parenting is not the character of your child. What gets in the way of parenting is one thing: the character of the parent. We turn God-given moments of ministry into reasons to be angry. We respond with impatience to moments where patience is required. We are self-righteous in moments where we're called to confess that we are more like our children than unalike. We throw threats at moments where quiet wisdom is what's needed. We take personal offense in places where we're being called to compassion and understanding. We're often mad at our children, not because they have broken God's law, but because they have gotten in the way of the laws of our peace and comfort. There are times when we are demanding when we should be serving. And sadly, there are moments when we are mad that our children need us to walk down the hall and parent them once more.

The kind of parenting that I have described in this chapter takes patience, humility, self-control, submission, gentleness, love, faithfulness, and joy. Let's be honest here: none of these character qualities are natural for us. It would be right for all of us to say, "If that's what's required to be a good parent, then I will never be one." But the good news is that we have not been left to our own strength and resources. Did you notice something about the list of character qualities that are necessary for us to be part of God's process in the lives of our kids? These character qualities all come out of Galatians 5:22–23. They are what's popularly known as the "fruit of the Spirit." I want you to think about these qualities with me for a moment.

If you view these character qualities as moral goals that you have been tasked to achieve, they will seem unattainable and discouraging to you. Here's the radical truth that as a parent you need to understand. These character qualities are not a moral standard that God lays before you and waits for you to achieve. No, they are the moral gifts of a God of glorious grace. What does this mean? It means that God knew that apart from his intervening work on our behalf, we wouldn't have a prayer of these character qualities ruling our hearts, and therefore, shaping our responses to our children. Not one of these characteristics is natural for sinners like you and me. Sin casts each of us not only into a moral drama, but a moral dilemma. What is the dilemma? It is that what God assigns to us, what he expects of us, and what he wants us to be part of, we are unable to do because we don't have the natural character to do it. But the good news is that the message of the Bible isn't that God puts an undoable standard before us and then sits by and judges us for our failures. No, the message is that God puts an uncompromising standard before us, then sends his Son to perfectly meet that standard on our behalf, so that we can be free to admit our failures and go to God for help. The cross of Jesus Christ means I don't have to deny my struggle as a parent, I don't have to act as if I'm something that I'm not, and I surely don't have to hide from the only One who is able to help me.

But there is more! The Galatians 5 passage teaches me that God blesses me not only with forgiveness, but also with new potential. Jesus died not only to forgive me, but by his grace to also transform me. The list of character qualities that we have been considering is our gift of his grace, given to every believer. Jesus died so that unloving people would become loving, complainers would become joyful, fighters would become peacemakers, impatient people would grow to be willing to wait, and unkind people would become those known for their kindness. Between the "already" of your conversion and the "not yet" of your home going, this is what God is working on in your heart and life. He works through all the mundane situations, locations, and relationships of your life to progressively transform you by his grace. Your heavenly Father has you in his process of grace so that you will have what you need to be part of his process of grace in the lives of your children. He parents you with patient mercy so that you'll be equipped to be able to parent your children with the same step-by-step grace that you are daily being given. And on the days when you are anything but patient, there are two things to remember. First, all of your failures have already been forgiven, so you can humbly admit them, confess them, and seek God's help. Second, you need to remember that you are not trapped in your cycle of failure because a God of abundant grace is at work changing, maturing, and growing you so that progressively you are more often part of what he wants to do in your children and less often in the way of it.

Like your children, you aren't left to parent yourself because God daily blesses you with his presence and grace, so that you can pass that same grace on to your children. Like you, they need to come to confess that they don't measure up. And because they don't measure up, they not only need your parental care, but even more importantly, they need the heavenly Father's life-long and heart-changing agenda of mercy.

$\mathcal{L}ost$

Principle: As a parent you're not dealing just with bad behavior, but a condition that causes bad behavior.

HERE'S A THOUGHT that has the ability to change the way you think about what God has called you to as a parent. It provides a very different way of interpreting those moments when your kids are driving you nuts or when they seem intent on resisting you. It will help you not to personalize things that at the core are not personal at all. This thought can keep you from allowing yourself to think that your son got up with the single-focused intention to wreck your day. It explains why you have to deal with things not just once, but over and over again. And this thought reinforces the significant spiritual nature of your role in the lives of your children.

Here's the thought that is vital to consider: in parenting you're not just dealing with your child's wrong *behaviors* but his *condition*. Perhaps you're thinking right now, "Paul, I don't have any idea what you're talking about. I just want my daughter to eat her carrots. I just want my son to pick up his clothes. I'm tired of my children arguing with me. I just want my kids to obey. If they did that, I would be satisfied." Here's what you need to understand. All of the resistance that you have to deal with, all of the fussing and complaining, all of the laziness and irresponsibility, all of the sibling squabbles, and all of the foolish choices, are the fruit of something deeper. If you don't understand that deeper thing, you will settle for surface victories and surface solutions that don't really lead to lasting change.

I often talk with exhausted and discouraged parents at parenting conferences. Some say, "I feel that nothing I do really works." Or they ask, "Why am I having to deal with the same thing over and over again?" Or they quietly confess that they can't wait for the day when the last child has left their home. I have many conversations with parents who in tears tell me that they have little relationship with their children. Or that they've read more than one parenting book and nothing has helped. I am deeply persuaded that when you don't know what you're dealing with, you become exhausted and discouraged with your "shot in the dark" attempts to deal with it.

So what does it mean to say that in parenting our kids we're not dealing just with behavior, but with a condition? One powerful sentence that came out of the mouth of the Messiah captures exactly what I'm talking about: *"For the Son of Man came to seek and to save the lost"* (Luke 19:10). You and I will never understand the task that God has called us to and the things that we deal with every day until we understand what Jesus means by these words. Our children are not just disobedient; they are disobedient because they are lost. Our children do not just make foolish choices; they make foolish choices because they are lost. Our children do not just have trouble getting along with their siblings; they have trouble getting along with their siblings because they are lost. Our children are not just lazy; they are lazy because they are lost. Our children don't just resist our authority; they resist our authority because they are lost. Everything that we're dealing with is the result of something deeper that must be in our understanding and focus.

Three Days of Good Behavior

She was very frustrated, and she wanted to let me know it. "Paul," she said, "I don't need a long parenting conference, with a bunch of dos and don'ts. Just give me three days of good behavior, and I would feel that I had died and gone to heaven!" I wasn't offended, because I'm a dad and I've personally felt her frustration. But her brief rant got me thinking. How many other parents are wishing for the same thing or say to their children, "Just behave, please!" They would almost do anything or pay anything or make any bargain necessary to get three days when their children were shining examples of self-initiated, noble behavior from early morning rise to lights out and in bed. But parenting is profoundly more than three days of good behavior or three years of good behavior or three decades of good behavior. Parenting is about the condition that makes good behavior seem such a hard and elusive goal.

Perhaps a medical example would help. If you were suffering from stomach cancer, you would be focused on the condition that you were dealing with, not just the symptoms of that condition. For example, you would celebrate three days free of intense abdominal pain and vomiting, but you wouldn't think that because you were blessed with three days of freedom from suffering that you were well. And you would know that medications that lessen your symptoms are a blessing because they allow you to be comfortable, but they do not offer you a solution. If you were living with stomach cancer, you would know that what you need help with and deliverance from is not just horribly uncomfortable symptoms, but the condition, cancer, that is the cause of every one of your symptoms. It would make no sense for you to attach yourself to a doctor who was great at alleviating symptoms, but had no understanding of the disease condition that is the cause of those symptoms.

So it is with parenting. Sure, you should always thank God for any moment when your child listens to you or chooses to do what is right. You should give thanks for those good days when your children are compliant and are getting along with one another. You should be thankful for any conversation that goes well and any situations where, if even for a brief moment, one of your children sees the light. You should be grateful for each time you are respected or when your children let you know they are thankful. You should be grateful for those times when the dinner meal is peaceful or your child's room is actually neat. But you mustn't be satisfied with these things. You mustn't allow yourself to think that these things are solutions. As a parent committed to being part of what God is doing in the lives of your children, you mustn't be content with alleviating symptoms while your children are suffering from a condition that is destructive to them and will be heartache to you.

So go ahead and celebrate those three days of good behavior, but don't let them satisfy your heart.

Your Children Are Lost. What Does That Mean?

Jesus uses the word *lost* in picturesque ways—the lost sheep, the lost coin, the lost son—and each of these gets at an element of what the condition "lost" means. *Lost* is one of those words that carries with it a variety of meanings. *Lost* can mean displaced; *lost* can mean dead; *lost* can mean defeated; and *lost* can mean confused. Three parables in the Bible capture what the biblical category of lost is all about. Understanding the focus of these three parables will help you begin to get a sense of who your children are and what God has called you to as a parent. Remember, your attention needs to be not only on the behavior of your child, but more fundamentally on the condition that produces that behavior. So, you can quit being reactive, but parent in those spontaneous moments with a sense of purpose and direction. Luke 15 is a tremendous help to parents, because, in vivid word pictures, it sheds light on the condition ("lost") that is the reason for all you have to deal with in the thoughts, desires, choices, words, and actions of your children.

The Parable of the Lost Sheep

Now the tax collectors and sinners were all drawing near to hear him. And the Pharisees and the scribes grumbled, saying, "This man receives sinners and eats with them."

So he told them this parable: "What man of you, having a hundred sheep, if he has lost one of them, does not leave the ninety-nine in the open country, and go after the one that is lost, until he finds it? And when he has found it, he lays it on his shoulders, rejoicing. And when he comes home, he calls together his friends and his neighbors, saying to them, 'Rejoice with me, for I have found my sheep that was lost.' Just so, I tell you, there will be more joy in heaven over one sinner who repents than over ninety-nine righteous persons who need no repentance."

The Parable of the Lost Coin

"Or what woman, having ten silver coins, if she loses one coin, does not light a lamp and sweep the house and seek diligently until she finds it? And when she has found it, she calls together her friends and neighbors, saying, 'Rejoice with me, for I have found the coin that I had lost.' Just so, I tell you, there is joy before the angels of God over one sinner who repents."

The Parable of the Prodigal Son

And he said, "There was a man who had two sons. And the younger of them said to his father, 'Father, give me the share of property that is coming to me.' And he divided his property between them. Not many days later, the younger son gathered all he had and took a journey into a far country, and there he squandered his property in reckless living. And when he had spent everything, a severe famine arose in that country, and he began to be in need. So he went and hired himself out to one of the citizens of that country, who sent him into his fields to feed pigs. And he was longing to be fed with the pods that the pigs ate, and no one gave him anything.

"But when he came to himself, he said, 'How many of my father's hired servants have more than enough bread, but I perish here with hunger! I will arise and go to my father, and I will say to him, "Father, I have sinned against heaven and before you. I am no longer worthy to be called your son. Treat me as one of your hired servants."' And he arose and came to his father. But while he was still a long way off, his father saw him and felt compassion, and ran and embraced him and kissed him. And the son said to him, 'Father, I have sinned against heaven and before you. I am no longer worthy to be called your son.' But the father said to his servants, 'Bring quickly the best robe, and put it on him, and put a ring on his hand, and shoes on his feet. And bring the fattened calf and kill it, and let us eat and celebrate. For this my son was dead, and is alive again; he was lost, and is found.' And they began to celebrate.

"Now his older son was in the field, and as he came and drew near to the house, he heard music and dancing. And he called one of the servants and asked what these things meant. And he said to him, 'Your brother has come, and your father has killed the fattened calf, because he has received him back safe and sound.' But he was angry and refused to go in. His father came out and entreated him, but he answered his father, 'Look, these many years I have served you, and I never disobeyed your command, yet you never gave me a young goat, that I might celebrate with my friends. But when this son of yours came, who has devoured your property with prostitutes, you killed the fattened calf for him!' And he said to him, 'Son, you are always with me, and all that is mine is yours. It was fitting to celebrate and be glad, for this your brother was dead, and is alive; he was lost, and is found.'" (Luke 15)

Each of these parables highlights an aspect of what it means to be lost and helps you to understand your experience with your children and your job description as their parent. Taking the parables in order, let's start with the lost sheep. Three things jump out of this parable. First, sheep need a shepherd. They need the wisdom, the protection, and the sustenance a shepherd can provide. Like your children, sheep were designed by the Creator to thrive under someone's care. You should never be irritated in those moments where it is clear that your children need you, no matter what it's interrupting. The fact that your children need to be supervised, cared for, and sustained by you is the wise choice of the Creator. Sheep need shepherding because they're sheep, and children need parenting because they're human beings. The needs of your children will get you up early in the morning, will interrupt you a hundred times during the day, and will even interfere with your sleep, but dependent is what they are and care is what God has called you to.

Second, sheep are prone to wander. It is in the nature of sheep to be easily distracted and quickly seduced by the lush green just beyond the borders of the fold. It is the nature of sheep to blindly follow another wandering sheep. So it is with your children. Because of the sin that lives inside them, children are prone to wander out of the protective instruction, correction, and discipline of their parents. They tend to be influenced by other children who are no more capable of guiding themselves than they are. Most of the wrong behavior of your children is not intentionally or self-consciously rebellious. Sometime it is, but most often their disobedience is the fruit of their lostness. Your son or daughter doesn't get up in the morning and say to him- or herself, "At 8:30 this morning I'm going to have an argument with Mom." Or, "At 7:30 tonight I'm going to find a way to directly disobey her." But when you interpret their disobedience this way, you tend to take their disobedience as personal and accuse them of things that were not in their heart. It's important to emphasize this point; your children will wander, and they'll do it not because they want to make war with you, but because they're lost.

But there's a third aspect to this evocative parable. Once a sheep has wandered, he is incapable of rescuing himself. He needs someone who will search for him, find him, and bring him home. So it is with your children. They don't so much need to be rescued from the world around them or from their friends; no, they need to be rescued from themselves. There is no greater danger in their lives then the danger they are to themselves. Why? Because they are lost, and in being lost they carry around inside them something that pulls them away from the care and protection that God has designed for them and that makes them think they can live more independently than any human being was designed to live. This means that parenting is a moment-by-moment, day-by-day rescue mission. It means that as parents we need to daily remind ourselves that we're called to rescue our children again and again, and we should not resent those moments when that rescue is necessary.

The parable of the lost coin is not about what it means for the coin to be lost; in this parable the spotlight is not on the coin, but on the one searching for it. This short little word picture, just three verses long, is a powerful portrayal of God's attitude toward the lost. Even though the woman still has nine coins, she intently searches for the one that is lost and when she finds it, she throws a party for her family and friends! This is the attitude of the heavenly Father, who cares about every one of his lost children, and when they are found, he throws a party with the angels in heaven. These three verses portray with power the compassion, the patience, and the grace that we are called to represent as God's ambassadors in the lives of our children. We're not mad at them because they're lost and need our help. We don't push their lostness in their faces. We don't remind them how much more righteous we are than they are, and that we would have never thought of doing and saying the things they do and say. No, we parent with mercy and grace. We live with them with patient hearts, and we celebrate every time they confess or choose to do what is right.

The longest of the three lost parables is the parable of the lost son. Perhaps the parable of the prodigal son is the best known of all of Christ's parables. An entire parenting book could be written out of this parable alone. Let's consider the ways this parable pictures what *lost* means and how it helps us to understand our job description as parents. Perhaps first you are hit with how intent this son is to be out on his own and to experience the world. His home offers him everything, but he cannot resist the temptation of independence. One of the scary components of the lostness of our children is their susceptibility to temptation. There is something inside them that hooks them to the dangerous things outside them. Again and again where you want your children to say no, they won't say no. But there is more. Coupled with the susceptibility to temptation is the tendency toward self-deception. What does this mean? The son in the parable told himself things about himself that were not true. He told himself he was able to handle what he could not handle. Likewise, your child is always talking to herself, and what she says to herself is profoundly important. Your child will tend to tell herself that she is able to do what no child is independently able to do.

All of this leads to the fact that lost people are a danger to themselves, and because they are, they are headed for destruction—although they probably don't know it. The danger that makes parenting both essential and difficult lives inside your child, not outside him. No child is free of that danger. The susceptibility to temptation and the tendency toward self-deception make your children a danger to themselves. Again, it is vital to understand that the rescue they need is rescue from themselves.

Finally, as the father in the story so powerfully demonstrates, what lost children need most is not criticism, judgment, condemnation, or punishment. Yes, children need authority. Yes, they need rules and the enforcement of those rules. Yes, they need to be held accountable for the choices that they make. But what I am going to say, I cannot emphasize enough; it is one of the central themes of this book. All of the things I just mentioned are important for protecting a child from himself, but they have no power whatsoever to deliver a child from himself, and every child needs that deliverance. Like the lost son, lost children need compassion, lost children need understanding, lost children need patience, lost children need acceptance, lost children need forgiveness, lost children need grace. It is stirring to see that the father of the lost son never gave up, he never gave way to bitterness and anger, he never threw away his hope, he never closed the door of his heart, and he never quit loving his son. He longed for and looked for and was ready for his son's return. What a beautiful parenting model for all of us. Now here's what you need to understand; the father in the story is the heavenly Father and the lost son is every one of us. Like our children, we are lost apart from God's rescue; like our children, we are susceptible to temptation; like our children, we are a danger to ourselves; like our children, we need the patient grace of our heavenly Father.

If all you had to deal with is the occasional bad behavior of your children, if all you had to do was regulate and control that behavior, parenting would be dramatically easier. But that's not all that you have to deal with. Every day, whether you've thought about it or not, you are confronted with the lostness of your children and how it causes them to resist authority, to want their own way, and to think they can do what they are not able to do. As I've already written in this book, rules don't have the power to deliver your children from this condition, but the powerful, transforming grace of God does. Parenting is about being a tool of that grace in the lives of our children.

Two Big Lies Every Lost Child Believes

It is important to understand that every child ever born believes two dangerous and destructive lies. If you pay attention, you can see these lies operating in the lives of your children. The power of these lies should be way more important to you than one bad and frustrating moment you experience with one of your children.

The first lie is the lie of *autonomy*. What this lie says is that I am a completely independent human being, and because I am, I have the right to live my life any way I choose to live it. It is the belief that my life belongs to me and that I should be able to do whatever I want with my life to make me happy. Part of this lie is the belief that no one should tell me what to do.

Parents who fight with a toddler about what to eat are not really fighting about what to eat. It's not that he has a different perspective on diet than you do. Come on, he knows nothing about diet. That fight is about autonomy. It's about that little boy's resistance to rules. It's about his belief that his little mouth belongs to him and no one will tell him what to put in it. My daughter decided she didn't want peas in her mouth. She had no intention of inserting green orbs into her oral cavity, although she had never tasted peas. So she would hold her jaw closed with the force of a pneumatic vice and would not open it. She was not defending herself against peas; she was defending her autonomy. She didn't know that no human being is designed to live independently.

The battle over what to wear is not a fight about fashion, but about autonomy. The fight about whether your teenage son can go to that party is not first about his deep commitment to the celebrations of his community of peers. That fight is about his continued resistance to being told what he can or cannot do. We all, including our children, resist being ruled. We all, including our children, want our own way. We all, including our children, set our minds on what we think will make us happy and get angry at anyone who stands in our way.

It's stunning to see the body of a child who is not yet able to talk stiffen in anger, not only because she is not getting her way, but because she already believes that it's her right to have her own way! It is shocking to see the amount of anger that comes out of a teenager when his mom says no to his weekend plans. He hates authority—not because he hates his parents, but because he believes that he is the only authority that he needs. Parents, every day you deal with the lie of autonomy operating in the hearts of your children; it's important to see beyond the issue of the moment. Don't settle for winning a battle about the thing, but rather each time fight for the heart behind the thing.

The second lie is equally dangerous. It is the lie of *self-sufficiency*. This lie tells your child that he has everything he needs inside himself to be what he needs to be and to do what he needs to do. He doesn't need your help, rescue, instruction, wisdom, or correction. It doesn't take long before you have to deal with the delusion of self-sufficiency in the heart of your child. A toddler has discovered that his shoes have laces that need to be tied. So he sits down and begins to fumble with his laces. He has no idea how to tie a bow. He could fumble with his laces for eternity and never end up with a bow, but when you reach down to help him, he slaps away your hand. That slap is not about lace ownership; it's about self-sufficiency. He desperately wants to believe that he can do quite well without your assistance or instruction. The teenage daughter who is arguing with you as you seek to impart to her some needed wisdom is arguing because she believes in her self-sufficiency, and because she does, she thinks she already has all the wisdom she needs.

No one is autonomous. No one is self-sufficient. Everyone needs parenting care. To believe anything else is to be dangerously deluded and headed for trouble. Parents, the scary thing is that our kids buy into both of these lies. You can see it in their actions, reactions, and responses.

So What Do Lost Children Need?
Lost children need:

1. *Insight.* The problem with lost children is that they don't see themselves as lost and because they don't, they don't understand how much they need your parenting care. So our children need not just to be told what to do, but they also need to be enabled to see. We need to look for ways to help them to understand the condition of danger that causes their behavior to be disruptive.
2. *Compassion.* It doesn't make any sense to get mad at somebody who is lost. It doesn't make any sense to make it a matter of personal offense against you. It doesn't make any sense to condemn a lost person with words or throw a punishment at them and walk away. Lost people need understanding and compassion. Lost children don't need parents who are irritated by their lostness, but rather who mourn it and long for them to be found.
3. *Hope.* As our children begin to admit the condition that they are in, and as they begin to own the danger they are to themselves, what they need to be assured of is that help is

available. They need to know that not only are we not their adversaries, we are their allies. We are here to do anything we can to protect, support, and guide them. But even more, they need to know that God sent his Son to earth so that when they begin to confess their need and cry out for help, they would have just the help that they need.

4. *Rescue.* Because of all that this chapter has discussed, parenting is not a behavior-control mission; it is a heart-rescue mission. The only hope for a lost child is a radical transformation of his heart. As parents, we have no ability to change our children's hearts, but the heavenly Father does, and we are his tools in the lives of our children. So we don't settle for the announcement of rules, the threat of punishment, and the enforcement of consequences. We are looking for every opportunity to address heart issues in our children, praying that as we do, God will work the change in them that only he can accomplish.

5. *Wisdom.* Our children need the wisdom to know when to say no. A successful life is all about saying no, but not to the authorities in your life, or to the people you've been called to love, or to God's call, but *no* to yourself. In our children's lostness they will think things that they should not think, they'll desire things they should not desire, and they will be pulled by dangerous emotions and seductive temptations. And if they don't learn when and how to say no, they will end up living as they were never intended to live.

So parents, what's the bottom line? Well, as Jesus came to seek and to save those who are lost, he calls us to love and to rescue our lost children. We don't give way to irritation, frustration, impatience, or discouragement. We move toward our children with the grace of forgiveness, wisdom, correction, and rescue, and we pray every day that God will empower our work as parents, and that he will change our children at that deepest of levels where every human being, including us, needs to be changed.

AUTHORITY

Principle: One of the foundational heart issues in the life of every child is authority. Teaching and modeling the protective beauty of authority is one of the foundations of good parenting.

SHE WAS IN TEARS as she spoke to me. Her frustration and dismay were written all over her face. She pushed through the crowd during a break at a weekend parenting conference. She was determined to talk to me, and it seemed nothing was going to stop her. She said, "I came here this weekend because I had to talk to you. You guys make parenting seem easy, with all your stories and principles, but it isn't easy. I have a four-year-old son who I cannot control. There is nothing that I can do or say that will make him obey me. And if I raise my voice and say no, he throws a fit and will not stop until I finally give him what he wants. Rather than me parenting him, I feel he is controlling me. I know it's wrong, but every morning I dread when he wakes up, and I can't wait for the evening when he goes to bed. In between is just battle after battle; nothing is easy or enjoyable. The new thing now is that if I even hint at saying no to him, he hits me. I know he's only four, but he has really hurt me a couple times. I'm at the end of my rope, and I don't know what to do."

How could your heart not go out to this poor, exhausted, discouraged, and frustrated woman? How could you not relate to how awful those battles are with a child that you love and you're trying to help? But I want you to stop and consider one phrase. I want you to let it sink in. "I have a four-year-old son who I cannot control." Four years old and he's already out of control. Four years old and he knows what to do to get his own way. Four years old and he has brought a thirty-two-year-old woman to the end of her rope. Four years old and his anger strikes fear into the heart of his thirty-two-year-old mother. Four years old and he sets the moral and relational agenda in his home. Four years old and his mother dreads the next day with him. Four years old and he sees his mother as an adversary, not a loving helper placed in his life by a loving God. Four years old and he sees authority as a very bad thing that he must fight at every point.

Now as you would probably understand, I couldn't give that dear mother the specificity she was hoping for, because in order to do that I would have to ask a whole lot of questions that would help me understand how things had gotten so bad. But I want to examine with you the significance of the issue that was at the center of the dysfunction between this tired mom and her angry son.

The Central Issue

What is going on between this mother and her son is deeper than moments of disrespect, deeper than defiant episodes, and deeper than a refusal to obey. All of these sad things are rooted in a very significant heart issue: authority. You could argue that if you don't deal with this fundamental heart issue, all the good things you seek to accomplish as God's tool in the life of your children will not work.

To begin with, it's important to always keep in mind that as a parent you are never just dealing with the words and actions of your children. You are always also dealing with the thing that shapes, directs, and controls the behavior of your children: the heart. I will say much more about this in the next chapter. And there is no more important heart issue for every child ever born than the issue of authority. Your children must learn early that they have been born into a world of authority, and they're not it. Why is this so important? Because submission to authority that is not me is unnatural for any sinner. Sin makes us want our own way. Sin makes us want to set our own rules. Sin convinces all of us that we know better. Sin causes me to want to do what I want to do when and how I want to do it. Sin makes me resist being told what to do by another. Sin really does insert me in the center of my world, the one place that I must never be because it is the place for God and God alone.

All of this means that children come into the world as self-appointed little self-sovereigns. That battle you have over the peas you want your daughter to eat is not about diet. Your three-year-old daughter is not saying to you, "I have studied my dietary needs, and it is not necessary that peas be included in a three-year-old's diet." No, this skirmish over something that is little in the scheme of things is not little at all because it is not about peas; it's about authority. Your daughter is saying to you, "No one but me will decide what I put in my mouth, thank you." Your daughter is not just resisting peas; she is fighting against the exercise of authority. She is fighting being told what to do. She is buying into the destructive delusion of self-rule.

The fights over when to go to bed, what to wear, what to watch on television, or the condition of the child's room are also not first about those issues; they are about this fundamental battle of the heart—who will decide how I will live? You can see this struggle even in a yet wordless infant. You've fed him. You've changed him. You've sung every song in your repertoire, and he's finally asleep. You begin tip-toeing out of the room, and just as you get to the door, you hear a bloodcurdling scream, and so you turn around. Your son has pushed himself up on his little arms, has stiffened his body, and is yelling for all he's worth. Do you know what he's saying in those unintelligible screams? "Oh no, you don't. You will not leave. I love you and have a wonderful plan for your life. I am the Lord!" He hasn't yet lived for two years, he can't even speak in real words, yet he wants to be, yes, is determined to be in charge.

Second Corinthians 5:15 is very helpful here: "And he died for all, that those who live might no longer live for themselves. . . ." Think of the significance of this statement. One of Jesus's primary purposes of going to the cross was to address the very thing that we are talking about. Jesus knew that your child would be born with a bondage to himself that only his grace could break. That drive to "live for himself" would make him all too self-focused and self-absorbed. It would make him angry at anything or anyone who would get in his holy way. It would make him shrink the focus of his concern, desires, and motives down to the small confines of his wants, his feelings, and his needs. And central to this sin-induced drive to live for himself is a hunger and a determination for self-rule.

This means there is a natural resistance to authority in every child who has ever been born since the fall of Adam and Eve in the garden. Every child in some way wants his or her own way. Every child tends to think that being told what to do is a negative thing. Every child wants to write his own moral rules and follow his own life plan. The delusion of the right to self-rule is one of the sad results of sin in the hearts of all of our children. But thankfully, this passage tells us way more than this. It tells you that as a Christian parent you are not alone in your battle to establish authority in the lives of your children. God controlled the forces of nature and ordered the events of human history so that at just the right time Jesus would come, live the life we could not live, die the death that we should have died, and rise again to defeat sin and death. He did all this so that by powerful delivering and transforming grace he would break our bondage to us.

Here's what this means. Mom and Dad, you have no ability at all—by the tone of your voice, by the force of your personality, by your physical size, or by your threats—to deliver your children from their addiction to self-rule. If you had that power, Jesus and his work would not have been necessary. But Jesus does have the power. He cares so much about the dark delusion of self-rule that lives in the hearts of all of our children that he literally gave his life so that they would be rescued and this bondage broken. Here's how important this is: People who are committed to self-rule won't submit to the rules of another, and because they won't submit to the rules of another, they won't think that they are wrong or confess their wrongs, and because they don't confess their wrongs, they won't seek God's forgiveness or seek God's help. You could argue that the drive for self-rule is the thing that, apart from God's grace, separates us and our children from God. You could not consider a more central heart issue for every child ever born than this one. To reject authority is to reject God, who is the authority over all authority, and rejection of God never has and never will go anywhere good.

The Gospel of Jesus Christ and Authority

So what 2 Corinthians 5:15 tells us is that your work to establish clear, loving, consistent, biblical authority in the lives of your children is doing gospel work. It is consistent with the gospel mission that brought Jesus to earth. It is at the center of what made the cross of sacrifice necessary. Authority work *is* grace work. Let's consider what that means. We will use Ephesians 6:1–4 to guide our discussion.

> Children, obey your parents in the Lord, for this is right. "Honor your father and mother" (this is the first commandment with a promise), "that it may go well with you and that you may live long in the land." Fathers, do not provoke your children to anger, but bring them up in the discipline and instruction of the Lord.

Exercising ambassadorial authority is doing gospel work. Please read the last sentence of the passage again. It's where our discussion of your exercise of authority must begin. It is vital that you understand that you have no independent, autonomous authority as a parent. None. You have not been given the right and power to exercise authority in the lives of your children any way you want; the opposite is true. The authority that you have is ambassadorial authority. The ambassador doesn't have any authority in and of himself. He has authority only because he represents a king who has authority. Here's God's amazing plan. He makes his invisible authority visible by sending visible authority figures as his representatives. This means that every time you exercise authority in the lives of your children, it must be a beautiful picture of the authority of God. In the lives of your children, you are the look of God's face, you are the touch of his hand, and you are the tone of his voice. You must never exercise authority in an angry, impatient way. You must never exercise authority in an abusive way. You must never exercise authority in a selfish way. Why? Because you have been put into your position as parent to display before your children how beautiful, wise, patient, guiding, protective, rescuing, and forgiving God's authority is.

This means you don't let your anger at your child's disobedience control you so you do things that you should not do (for example, pinching, poking, yanking, slapping, shoving your child). It means that you never combine your discipline with berating, demeaning, or condemning talk. ("What are you, stupid?" "I can't believe that you're my daughter!" "I've forgotten more than you'll ever know!") It means you don't treat your child as your indentured servant, there to make your life easier. (Yes, your child should participate in the chores of the house, but if you're a father who likes to read the newspaper and it is five steps from you, don't call your son who is upstairs to come downstairs and get it for you.) You should never exercise authority in a way that makes it look as though you're breaking relationship with your child. You should never let your exercise of authority be dictated by your mood. (This will always lead to a confusing and inconsistent culture of authority, where what was wrong yesterday doesn't seem so wrong today. In this kind of unpredictable, insecure environment, children become emotional weathermen, nervously gauging the weather of their parents to see what they can or cannot do without getting in trouble.)

Why is this so important? It's important because, as I said earlier, your children enter the world resistant to authority. They don't tend to see that real life is found inside a life of willing submission to authority. If you exercise authority in a lazy, abusive, selfish way, you will deepen and strengthen the natural rebellion to authority in the hearts of your children. What God has called you to is to daily confront your children with how beautiful, helpful, and patient God's authority is. You want to be used of God to help your children to begin to believe that submission to authority is where life and freedom are to be found. When this happens, children begin to admit their need, confess their wrongs, and reach out for the help of the Savior. Nothing in your child's life is more important than this. *What kind of picture are your children getting of God's authority by the way you exercise yours?*

Helping your children to understand why they do what they do is doing gospel work. Please read that last sentence of the passage one more time. Notice that you are called not just to "discipline" but also to "instruction." Here's the bottom line. Your children don't have a clue why they do the things they do. They don't know why they resist you. They don't know why they argue with you. They don't know why you make them angry. They don't know why they think that they know better than you. They don't know why they demand their own way. They don't know why they will put themselves through tension and painful situations in order to fight for a little independence. Your children don't know who they are and why they do the things they do. Your children daily suffer from a lack of spiritual self-understanding.

Parents, that's our job. It is never enough, when your child has done something wrong, to just mete out discipline, because you're always dealing with something deeper than just behavior. Your discipline must every time be coupled with clear biblical instruction.

I don't mean angry sermons. What I mean is a brief conversation that once again enables your child to look at, examine, and understand the heart struggle behind his authority resistance. In his Word, God has revealed to you the mysteries of human desire and motivation so that you can then reveal those mysteries to your children who are lost, ignorant, and deceived. Every time you couple ambassadorial discipline with ambassadorial instruction, you are giving the Spirit of God another opportunity to work conviction and desire for help into the heart of your children. The more your children understand why they do what they do, the easier it will be for them to admit their wrongs and seek your forgiveness and God's. Remember, because everything they do comes out of their hearts, everything they do reveals their hearts. Helping your children see what their behavior reveals about their hearts is gospel work. *How often do you combine moments of discipline with patient, insight-giving instruction?*

Establishing authority early in little things is doing gospel work. Fight your authority battles early. Fight them when the issues are small. Capitalize on the little moments God will give you when your children are still young. You do not want to be fighting authority battles with a seventeen-year-old. Don't tell yourself that those little moments of resistance to your authority (what to eat, what to wear, when to go to bed, what to watch, doing chores, etc.) are unimportant because the issue at hand is not that important. Those little moments are profoundly important because, as I stated earlier, the resistance is not coming from their thoughts about food or sleep, but from hearts that will tend to resist all authority but their own.

Be thankful for these little moments. Don't look at them as the bad moments of parenting, as hassles and interruptions; these are the good moments of parenting. These are moments of grace. This brings us to another one of the basic themes of this book. Parents, if your eyes ever see or your ears ever hear the sin and weakness of your children, it's never an accident, it's never a hassle, it's never an interruption; it's always grace. God loves your children and because he does, he has placed them in a family of faith so that you can be his tool of convicting, forgiving, and transforming grace. You are faced with the resistance of your children because God is a God of amazing grace. His grace has the power to turn very bad moments into the very good moments. Isn't this what the cross of Jesus Christ is about? The cross is the worst thing that ever happened that, by God's plan, became the best thing that ever happened. God inhabits your trials of discipline with his presence and grace to do in those moments in the hearts of your children what you would never be able to do. Don't get mad in those moments; don't be frustrated that you have to deal with the same thing over and over again. Thank God for his grace and seek to be a tool in his powerful hands.

But there's another thing that needs to be said about these little moments of discipline and instruction while your children are still young. Know that your children do not know what true obedience looks like. It's your job to clarify this for them. What is obedience? It's a willing submission of my heart to the authorities that God has placed in my life. What does this willing submission of the heart do? It causes me to be motivated to and find joy in doing what the authorities that God has placed in my life have asked me to do. Here's what this means. If you ask little Sharon to go down the hallway and into her room and pick up the toys that she has scattered everywhere, and she is yelling at you as she goes, it is very important that you do not let Sharon think that she is obeying you. Because even though you can see Sharon's body moving toward her room, her heart is raging in anger and rebellion against you and against your authority. True obedience always begins with the heart.

So you need to call Sharon back, not to say, "Don't you ever dare talk to me that way again. Who do you think you are! Look at the size of me and the size of you. You don't want to think about what will happen to you if you ever talk to me that way again!" You see, that kind of angry response hardens Sharon's heart against authority, when what you want to do is be used of God to soften it. You need to quickly pray for patience and grace and then lovingly call Sharon back and say, "Sharon, we have a problem here. Mommy wasn't unkind to you. Mommy didn't ask you to do something bad. Mommy didn't call you mean names, yet you're yelling at Mommy. When you yell at Mommy, you are trying to be the mommy of Mommy, and if you're the mommy of Mommy, then you have no Mommy over you to guide and protect you." Will your daughter immediately fall to her knees and say, "I get it; I am a self-oriented rebel against authority. I want to rule my own world and so I hate being told what to do. Mommy, I need to be rescued from the danger I am to myself!" Of course, that won't happen, but you have taken one little step in helping your daughter to understand her heart, and you will have many, many more conversations like this, capturing little moments that God will empower by his grace. *Did you fight or are you fighting your authority battles early? If not, what changes in the way you look at little moments of discipline need to take place in you and the way you respond to your children?*

Exercising consistent authority is doing gospel work. I talked about this earlier, but here are a few more thoughts. The exercise of God's love never gets in the way of the exercise of his authority. The dispensing of God's grace never compromises God's exercise of his authority. The accomplishing of God's sovereign plan is never interrupted by his exercise of authority. God doesn't get tired of enforcing his rules. He doesn't have bad days when he's angrier and meaner. His divine joy doesn't keep him from doing the hard work of being a faithful disciplining father; the opposite is true. God is glorious in the utter consistency of his faithfulness to uphold his holy commands and to discipline his children. So we too must be like him as his ambassadors. Our children need the security of faithful, consistent, firm, uncompromising, and loving authority—authority that is motivated by and tempered by grace. *Is your exercise of parental authority consistent because it's driven by God's call or is it inconsistent because it's shaped by the emotion of the moment?*

Confessing that when it comes to authority you are more like your children than unlike them is doing gospel work. Why do we get angry when we exercise authority, why do we make a big deal of something one day and then blow if off the next, and why do we tend to look at discipline moments as hassles? We do all of these things because we are more like our children than unlike them. Sin is inside us just as it's inside them, and it causes us to want our own way and to want to do things our way, just as it does with our children. You see, anytime we exercise ambassadorial authority in a mean, angry, impatient, condemning, or abusive way, we are rebelling against the authority of the One we have been called to represent. It's not just our children who have an authority problem; we do too. It's not just our children who need patient rescue; we do too. It's not just our children who need insight-giving instruction; we do too. It's not just our children who need forgiving grace; we do too. It's not just our children who obey with their bodies but still harbor rebellion in their hearts. Our anger and impatience as parents reveal the true condition of our hearts. Like our children, we need the care of a loving Father who doesn't beat us with condemnation, but rather caresses us with his grace. Who could understand the call to make his authority visible and say, "Yeah, I can do that, no problem"? Understanding the profound holiness of God's call confronts us with the profound depth of our inadequacy. You see, it's essential to confess this, because no parent gives grace more joyfully and consistently than the parent who daily confesses that she desperately needs it herself. God calls rebels to his authority to rescue rebels against his authority. Only powerful grace can make that happen. *Do you humbly own the rebellion of your own heart as you deal with the rebellion of your children in a way that causes you to exercise authority with patience and grace?*

In discussions of authority, talking about the cross of Jesus Christ is doing gospel work. If Jesus came and died to break the bondage of our hearts and our children's hearts to our independent authority, and in so doing, to rescue us from us, it's not weird to talk about the gift of the cross of Jesus Christ in moments of discipline. It's not weird to talk about the forgiveness and hope of change that the cross provides. In fact, it's weird not to. Were it not for sin, there would be no rebellion; were it not for rebellion, there would be no need for a Savior; and were it not for the need of a Savior, there would have been no need for the cross. So every moment of rebellion reveals a child's heart, and every moment when a child's heart is revealed is a God-given opportunity to talk about the Savior who alone can deliver this child from himself. It is important to again and again embed the story of your child's rebellion into the larger story of redemption. *In moments of discipline, do you often point your children to the hope and help that is to be found in the life, death, and resurrection of Jesus?*

It really is true that there is no more central issue in the lives of our children. Their struggle with authority really does reveal the depth of the hold of sin on their hearts and their need for the grace of the Savior. And in that way we really are like our children. When we admit that, we are able to exercise authority with humility and grace, giving our children a little picture of how gloriously beautiful and good God's authority actually is.

9

Foolishness

Principle: The foolishness inside your children is more dangerous to them than the temptation outside of them. Only God's grace has the power to rescue fools.

SALLY HAS DECIDED at two-and-a-half years old that she will never eat vegetables in her entire life.

Billy is five and has told his parents he won't sleep if he cannot sleep with them.

Jared argues with his dad every time he's told what to do.

Cindy is six and thinks it's dumb that she can't wear makeup yet.

Bo really does think that his future is in video games and not in doing homework.

Miley is obsessed with sending silly texts to friends during school.

Jason doesn't think that smoking pot is such a big deal.

Sarah lies whenever it seems necessary to her.

Jennifer is simply obsessed with her appearance.

Peter thinks that sports are the most important thing in his life.

Justin has blown off high school and crushed his chances at going to college.

These are all kids of various ages and in different situations, but the same theme runs through all of their stories. It is the thing that their parents bump into every day. It is the thing that is of greatest danger to them. It's the thing that will complicate their lives more than they know. It's the thing that brings repeated conflict into their relationship with their parents. This thing is not first about something they did. No, it's about who they are. They came into the world with it and they have no ability to free themselves from it, and so they need to be rescued out of it. It's that sad and dangerous thing the Bible calls *foolishness*. I am deeply persuaded that if you don't understand what the Bible says about foolishness, you won't fully understand what God has called you to as his instrument in the lives of your children.

It's All about the Heart

Here's where we need to begin. As a parent you are never, ever dealing just with the words and actions of your children. You are always also dealing with the thing that controls their words and behavior: the heart. Sadly, many Christian parents lose sight of this or don't know this, so they think that their job is to direct and control their children's behavior. So they spend all of their parental focus and energy on announcing and enforcing the law. Now, as I've already said in this book, your children need law and they need authorities that announce it and enforce it, but they need much, much more. The law has a very powerful ability to reveal the sin that lives inside your children, and the law is God's perfect guide for your children's living, but the law has no ability to change them. The law will not make them want to do what is right. The law won't make them humble worshipers of God. The law won't free them from their arrogance and self-worship. The law won't make them righteous. The law is a very good thing, but not enough of a thing.

As a Christian parent, you must carry with you, in a way that shapes your parenting, a practical theology of the heart. This biblical theology of the heart must guide you as you interact with the misbehavior of your children. You may be thinking, "Paul, I get what you're saying, but I don't know what that looks like as I deal with my children every day." This is precisely where a little verse in the opening chapters of Proverbs can not only give you insight, but can transform the way you think about what God has called you to be and do in the lives of the children he has entrusted to your care. Read carefully and repeatedly the words of Proverbs 4:23. Remember, what you are about to read are the words of counsel a wise father is giving to his son: *"Keep your heart with all vigilance, for from it flow the springs of life."*

What does the father mean when he says to his son, "Keep your heart with all vigilance"? Well, what he's saying is, "Son, if you pay attention to anything, pay attention to this. Focus on this. Make this a priority. Don't get distracted and forget this." What is the *this*? The *this* is the heart. Why would a wise father say, "Son, be very, very careful to always pay attention to the content and character of your heart"? Why is this such an important thing for a wise father to communicate to his son? Why is it such an important thing for his son to hear? Before I answer the questions I have proposed, I want to make a rather sad observation. There are thousands and thousands of Christian parents who never would think of saying this to one of their children. There are thousands and thousands of Christian parents who have never had a heart-focused conversation with one of their children. So why in the wisdom conversation this father is having with his son, is this the main thing that he wants to say?

The answer to the question that is posited in the first half of Proverbs 4:23 is answered by the second half of the same verse. "Son, pay careful attention to your heart." Why? Because "from it flow the springs of life." What does that mean? It means that the life of your children is controlled by their hearts. This means that the words and behavior of your children flow out of whatever is in their hearts. Here's a biblical definition of the heart: *the heart is the causal core of your child's personhood.* It's the heart that causes your children to do and say what they do and say. Like us, our children live out of their hearts. Like us, their words and behavior are more shaped by what's inside them than what's outside them. This means that whatever rules their hearts will control their words and actions.

This means that all of your children's word problems are first heart problems. The mean things they say to one another begin with hatred, anger, bitterness, selfishness, jealousy, unkindness, impatience, or a lack of love in their hearts. The disobedience that you deal with is not first a behavioral problem; it is a heart problem. Your children disobey because of the pride, rebellion, autonomy, self-sufficiency, and desire for self-rule that control their hearts. It's not enough to say no or "Because you did this, this is what you're going to get."

If parenting must include and focus on the heart, here are two things that you must always keep in mind. First, you must remind *yourself* again and again, so that in the press of the duties of parenting you don't forget that all of your children's behavior problems are heart problems. Yes, it is true; it is the heart that is the problem (both your children's and yours). The second thing you must call yourself to remember is that lasting change in the behavior of your children (the thing that all parents long for) will always travel through the pathway of the heart. If the heart of your child does not change, his behavior won't change for very long. This means that every moment of discipline and correction must be accompanied with instruction. And what kind of instruction? When you're disciplining your child, you are being afforded a God-given opportunity to talk about his heart. Since it is true that his behavior reveals the true condition of his heart, his misbehavior gives you a picture of what controls his heart, and you have been given an opportunity by your Savior of grace to help the child see what is in his heart. Each time you do this, you are part of what God is seeking to do in the life of your child, and you are giving the Spirit of God an opportunity to impart self-knowledge to your child, including a sense of wrong, personal conviction, and a desire to change. In these moments ask questions, tell stories, give illustrations—anything you can do to get the child to step out of himself, to quit defending himself, and to look into and examine his heart.

These moments are not so much "legal" moments, where the emphasis is on the rules and the punishment that is coming for breaking the rules, but on how a God of love is using all of it to help our children see themselves, admit what they see, and reach out for God's help. This means that these "law" moments are actually "grace" moments, and when you get that, it transforms what you do as you deal with your children. You don't *threaten* them: "You just don't want to think about what I am going to do if I have to break up one more fight today!" You don't *manipulate* your children: "If you're nice to your sisters all next week, I'll buy you that Star Wars action figure you've been asking for." You don't try to make your children feel *guilty*: "I remember when our lives were simple. Now everything gets complicated by the way you behave." Threat, manipulation, and guilt are tools that parents use to produce change in their children without having to deal with the heart.

This is where the gospel of Jesus Christ that we say we believe is helpful for our parenting. Listen to the bright, golden promise of the work of the Savior that is yet to come: "I will give you a new heart, and a new spirit I will put in you. And I will remove the heart of stone from your flesh and give you a heart of flesh" (Ezek. 36:26). Jesus came to give us and our children the one thing that we all desperately need—a new heart. This means that the focus of the life, death, and resurrection of Jesus is not first new behavior, but a renewed heart, because if our hearts are not renewed, our behavior will never change.

Now, what does a "new heart" mean? It doesn't mean a perfect heart. Notice the word picture of the difference between stone and flesh. As I wrote earlier, if I had a stone in my hands and squeezed it with all of my might, what do you think would happen? Well, the only logical answer is, nothing. That stone is hard, and because it is hard, it's resistant to change. Flesh is soft, and because it's soft, it's moldable or capable of change. Jesus came so that our hearts would be new and renewing. He came so our hearts would change and be changing. This is what he wants for our children. That is why he will expose the hearts of our children to us, so that we can be tools of his work of change. Why is this prophecy about Jesus in the Old Testament? It's there to remind us that lasting heart change is impossible apart from his rescuing, forgiving, transforming, and delivering grace. Without this grace our children are cursed to live with the stony hearts they were born with, and we are forced to parent without any real hope of lasting change.

But God hasn't left us without the help of his grace. He sent his Son so that it would be practically possible for us to be instruments of real and lasting heart change in our children. Once you understand this, then you begin to also understand that every moment of discipline and correction is at the same time a God-given opportunity to get at issues of the heart with our children. Your children need your authority, but they also need the grace of insight, because the grace of insight is the doorway to the grace of confession, which is the doorway to the grace of new life.

Another observation that I want to make is that understanding what the Bible says about the heart exposes the inherent weakness and inadequacy of what I call *monastic parenting*. Think with me for a moment about the theology that resulted in the building of medieval monasteries. The thinking was that there's an evil world out there, and the way to escape that evil is to create a community that lives inside a big wall that separates you from that evil of the surrounding world. The problem is that in little ways and big ways the monasteries that were built struggled with all the same things that they were trying to escape. What was the big mistake that monasteries made? I can tell you; they let people in them! And people brought with them all the evils of their own hearts. You see, culture isn't the problem, people are. It's people that cause a culture to be morally wrong and morally dangerous.

Yet, many Christian parents think that the main thing they need to do to produce children who are what God wants them to be is to protect their children from the evils of the surrounding culture. Should your children be exposed to all that our culture has to offer? The answer is obvious: "Absolutely not!" Do they constantly need your wise protection? Again, the answer is obvious: "All the time!" But God has not called us to erect a little family monastery. Please read carefully what I am going to write next. Monastic parenting will not deliver your children from moral danger. What the Bible has to say about the heart, which we have been considering, tells you why. The Bible tell us again and again that the greatest danger to us and our children lives inside us and not outside us. It's the sin, iniquity, and transgression of our hearts and our children's hearts that is the biggest moral danger to us. That is why we all need the grace of a new heart, and that is why protective (monastic) parenting is inadequate. You will never build walls of protection that protect your children from the danger that resides in their own hearts. So protect your children; you must because you live in a fallen world. But know that doing this is only a small part of the greater heart work that God has called you to.

If the Heart Is the Problem, Then What Is the Problem with the Heart?

The Bible is very clear about the dysfunction in the heart of every child, and understanding what the Bible says will change the way you think about parenting those that God has entrusted into your care. To understand what is wrong inside the hearts of your children, we look again to Proverbs: "Folly is bound up in the heart of a child, but the rod of discipline drives it far from him" (Prov. 22:15). Folly (foolishness) is what you deal with as a parent every day whether you know it or not. Foolishness is what makes your child think he knows better than you do. Foolishness is what makes her rebel against your authority. Foolishness is what makes siblings constantly fight with one another. Foolishness is what makes a teenager think the world's way is better than God's way. Foolishness is what makes a child think it is better to get out of work than to faithfully do his work. Foolishness is what makes a child think that material things are more important than spiritual things. It is foolishness that makes your job as a parent both essential and difficult.

Rather than being unkind, it is in fact biblical to look at your children and to understand that you are parenting fools. It is vital to understand that this foolishness is one of the chief dangers that your children face. And foolishness is a danger they cannot escape, because it resides in their hearts. Fools need help. Fools need rescue. Fools need to understand the danger they are to themselves. Fools need to change.

You may be asking yourself right now, "What is foolishness, anyway?" The fool has the world inside out and upside down. The fool looks at what is foolish and sees it as wise. The fool looks at what is good and sees it as bad. The fool looks at what is false and sees it as true. The fool hates to be ruled by another. The fool hates to have to stay inside of boundaries. The fool wants his own way. The fool looks at others as being in the way. The fool doesn't think he needs to learn. The fool thinks he is always right. The fool lives for what is fading rather than for what is eternal. The fool puts himself in the middle of things and makes it all about him. The fool demands to be served and hates to have to serve. The fool argues with the wise and listens to other fools. The fool has it all wrong, but is convinced he is always right. The fool walks the path of danger and destruction, but thinks he has the good life. The words of Proverbs are tragic. They should break your heart. Your child has the heart of a fool and because he does, he is a danger to himself and desperately needs God's arms of rescue that come through your parenting care.

But you cannot really understand either the source or danger of the foolishness that is in the heart of every child without the words of Psalm 53:

The fool says in his heart, "There is no God."
>They are corrupt, doing abominable iniquity;
>there is none who does good.
God looks down from heaven
>on the children of man
to see if there are any who understand,
>who seek after God.
They have all fallen away;
>together they have become corrupt;
there is none who does good,
>not even one. (Ps. 53:1–3)

The epicenter of the foolishness that is in the heart of every child is deeply theological. Most Christian parents fail to understand this. The struggles over food, sleep, homework, sibling conflict, possessions, wardrobe, and dating are theological struggles. You see, at the center of the foolishness of the children you are called to parent is a denial of God. I don't think that passage is talking about formal philosophical atheism (although it would include that). At street level what this passage is talking about is the propensity of our children to live as if God doesn't exist. This denial of God is living without a sense of need for his authority, wisdom, power, and grace. It's about inserting myself in the center. It's about the propensity of our children to make their happiness the most important thing in the universe. It's denying God's right to rule and the wisdom of his rules. And when I deny God in this way, I will not appreciate the authorities he has placed in my life and I will not want to submit to the boundaries that God and those authorities place around me. So I will be attracted to what is wrong and do things that I should not do. Because this foolishness is in the heart of every child, the psalmist says, "There is none who does good; not even one" (v. 3). It is important to remember that you can say that you believe in God, but practically deny his existence in the way that you live every day.

Parents, here's what you have to understand. It is more natural for your children to deny God's existence than it is for them to humbly recognize it and submit to his holy demands on their lives. It is more natural for your children to be happy in setting themselves up as God, than to willingly and joyfully submit to the one who is God. No wonder that they resist your authority. No wonder they argue with you even though you clearly know more and better. No wonder they're in constant conflict with one another. No wonder they are entitled, demanding, easily bored, and often unthankful. No wonder you are exhausted at the end of the day. No wonder you get discouraged with the process. Sin reduces all of our children to fools (us too) and because it does, it causes them to live as if God doesn't exist, and because they do that, they will be attracted to what is wrong and resist when you ask them to do what is right. It is a simple but sad equation. If you do not submit to God's way, you will want your own way. This defines the struggle of our children and the daily job description of those who parent them.

So How Do You Parent a Fool?

Right away you have to recognize that what we're considering right now exposes the fundamental inadequacy of reducing Christian parenting down to rules and regulations that are clearly announced and faithfully enforced. Rules are a great protection for your child, but no rule has the power to deliver your child from his foolishness. Here is the spiritual paradox that every Christian parent needs to understand: The only hope for a fool is the God that every fool somehow, someway denies. The only hope for a fool is God's amazing, rescuing, forgiving, transforming, and delivering grace. This means that as parents we are called to be representatives not only of God's holy authority, but also of his redeeming grace.

Here's the rub. We all tend to be better at enforcing the law than we are at extending grace. What does it look like to be visible extenders of God's invisible grace in the lives of our children? I want to answer the question with the four words that follow. You should carry these four words with you every day as do your parenting work, because these four words represent the rescue and salvation of a fool.

1. Glory

The only solution to your child's addiction to his own glory is to introduce him to a greater glory. Human beings were meant to live in a life-shaping awe of the existence and glory of God, and when we don't, we don't live in the way that we were designed to live. Our job as a parent is to open the eyes of our children to the stunning glory of God. Our job is to help our children to be so blown away by God's glory that they find joy in submitting to his rule.

Now, God has helped us by creating a world that reveals his glory everywhere you look. God intentionally designed his world to reveal himself, because he knows how easy it is for us to be blind to his existence. Therefore it's not unnatural to talk about God all the time, because he's everywhere to be seen. How can you boil an egg, see the rising sun, hear the pounding of the rain, listen to the song of a bird, listen to the sizzle of a steak, watch the falling of the winter's snow, view the turning of the leaves, stand on a beach and gaze across the seemingly endless ocean, listen to the huge catalog of different-sounding human voices, and not talk to your children about the glory of God? Every day God will give you theological opportunities, moments to help your children see the one thing they desperately need to see. *The question is, Are you capturing these glory moments with a mission to rescue your children from their foolishness?*

2. Wisdom

It's pretty obvious that what a fool needs is wisdom. As a parent of a fool, you need to be looking for wisdom moments. God will give you opportunities every day to point to how beautiful, protective, practical, helpful, and good God's wisdom really is. Think about it. Who wouldn't want to live in a world where everyone was kind, loving, humble, patient, giving, and serving? Who wouldn't want to live in a world where no one ever stole anything, where no one ever took another person's wife, where there was no violence or murder, where no one was ever jealous or eaten by envy, where governments weren't corrupt, and where people were always truthful? I have just described the world that God in his wisdom wants for us.

It is important to understand that since your children do not come into the world hungering for God's wisdom, as a parent you have to be committed to be a salesman for it. You have to be committed to daily selling to your children what they're not seeking, and you do that by showing your children how beautiful it is. So don't be mad when you have to discipline your children. A God of grace is giving you an opportunity to be part of his rescue of them. Patiently capture those moments, not just by enforcing the rules, but by talking about how gorgeous God's wise way is.

3. Story

As you are doing this, tell the story of the person and work of Jesus to your children again and again and again. Tell them how God could have condemned us all to our foolishness and its results, but instead how he sent his Son so that instead of being condemned, we'd be forgiven and rescued from ourselves. You simply cannot tell this story to your children enough. Talk about how God exercised his power to control history so that at just the right time Jesus would come and extend his sacrificial love to fools who didn't even recognize his existence. Talk to them about how Wisdom came to rescue fools so that fools would become wise. Start telling this story when they are toddlers and don't stop telling this story until your young adult children have left your home.

4. Welcome

Finally, talk about how God right here, right now, extends a welcome to them to confess their foolishness, to seek his forgiveness, and to receive his eternal help. Talk to them about how Jesus lived a perfectly righteous life so that unrighteous people could be welcomed into the arms of a perfectly holy God. And tell them that when he extends his forgiving grace to them, he will not turn his back on them ever again, no matter how foolish they are. Don't yell at your children; lead them to confession. Be a visible representative of the patient and forgiving welcome that God extends to all who come to him.

Parenting is about parenting the heart, and parenting the heart means recognizing and dealing with the foolishness that is in the hearts of all of our children. This confronts us with the fact again that our children don't just need God's law; they are also born with a deep, abiding need for his grace, and we are called to be tools of that grace in the hearts and lives of our children.

One more thing needs to be said. If you want to be God's tool of heart rescue and heart change in the lives of your children, you have to be humbly willing to start with your own heart. It is true that your heart will cause you to be in the way of what God is doing rather than being a willing part of it. Let's say that it's 10:30 p.m. and the children you put to bed at 9:00 p.m. are now fighting in their beds. You start down the hallway with feet heavy on the floorboards. You're probably not saying, "Thank you, God, for this wonderful opportunity to rescue my children from the foolishness that is so dangerous to them. I love your grace." You're probably saying, "They're dead!" And you're about to go into their room and in anger do and say things that you should not do or say. Now think with me: Why are you angry? I would propose to you that you're not angry that your children have broken God's law, because that would be the anger of wisdom, correction, and grace. You're angry because your children have broken your law, and in your system of law, there shall be no parenting after 10:00 p.m.

Now, I'm about to hurt your feelings. When we go off and rip into our children, we are responding as a fool. A fool turns moments of ministry into moments of anger. A fool personalizes what is not personal. A fool is adversarial in these moments in his responses. And a fool settles for quick solutions that do not get to the heart of the matter. Sadly, I was that fool many times with my children. You see, getting at the foolishness that is in the heart of all of our children begins with us confessing that we're fools too. It's not just our children who need rescue. It's not just our children who forget God and do foolish things. It's not just our children who want their own way. It's not just our children who make it all about them. We do all of these things too and because we do, our daily need for God's rescue and forgiveness is just as great as our children's is.

The mystery of the way God works is that he sends fools to rescue fools and because he does, it takes grace to be a tool of God's agenda of rescuing grace. Parents, the more you are ready and willing to confess the foolishness that causes you to need God's grace, the more you will be willing and ready to extend that grace to the foolish hearts of the children he has entrusted to your care. But remember: because of what Jesus has done for us, that grace is ready for the taking right here, right now.

Character

Principle: Not all of the wrong your children do is a direct rebellion to authority; much of the wrong is the result of a lack of character.

LET ME PLAY OUT a scene for you. It's Tuesday late afternoon at the Siths'. They live in an open floor plan house, where the kitchen, living room, and family room all meld into one another. Mom is in the kitchen, and she is in full-blown, nervous, and frenetic mode because in an hour or so a family of six is going to arrive for dinner and she is not remotely near being ready. In the family room, in full sight of Mom, are her three children, ages 7, 9, and 11, and they are playing Wii bowling together. Now, think with me carefully as I ask the following question: What is wrong with this scene?

I would imagine many of you would answer, "Nothing! If I'm working as fast and hard as I can to get something done and my children are quietly playing together, Jesus has surely visited my house!" But at closer examination, what is being revealed in this moment in the lives of these children is a very important lack of character. Each of these children is old enough to understand that their mom is up against it. Each of them has become accustomed to sensing her emotions. Each of them is able to understand that she needs help. And each of them is in possession of skills to help her, and in helping her, lift some of the pressure that she is feeling. But not one of them offers help, because they don't actually care. They don't care that she is nervous and discouraged. They don't care that she is hurt that they don't offer to help. They don't care that she may be embarrassed in front of her friends. They don't care.

You wouldn't want such a person as your friend. You wouldn't want such an uncaring person as your spouse. You wouldn't want such an unfeeling person as your neighbor or your boss. What God is graciously revealing in the hearts of these children is not okay in them, and it should not be okay to us. What is being revealed is the source of much of the hurt, heartache, dysfunction, and conflict in the human community. So, it's not enough to target the direct disobedience of your children; as a parent you must also have an eye toward their character.

You see, in the situation that I have described, the children have not rebelled against a rule. They have not disobeyed their mom's command. They have not refused to do what they are told. But what they are doing is wrong in the eyes of God, and it should be seen as wrong by us as well. The problem with these children is not that they have conspired together to rebel against their mother. Their problem is that they lack character and because they do, they haven't done what is right, good, loving, and kind. You will miss God-given opportunity after God-given opportunity if you do not understand that not every wrong thing your child does is a direct rebellion to authority. Much of the wrong they do is the result of a lack of character.

It's not enough to just emphasize the beauty of submission to authority. You must also emphasize the need for character development. In both of these you're helping your children to recognize and understand the damage that sin does to their hearts and to ours as well. Now, you don't march into the family room, stand in front of the flat-screen, and start yelling at your children: "How dare you watch me be so upset and not offer to help me after all the things I've done for you! I want you to unplug the game machine and hand it to me. Take a good look at it because you'll never see it again! Children that are as cold and unfeeling as you don't deserve a game machine! Now, get your rear ends into the kitchen as fast as you can and do what I tell you to do or, well, you don't want to know what will happen!" What I'm saying is this: if you deal with a lack of character with a lack of character, you will not accomplish what God has given you to accomplish in the hearts of your children.

Proper handling of these kinds of situations always begins not with a lecture, but with confession. Before you talk to your children, you and I need to talk to ourselves and to our Lord. We need to confess that it's not just our children who lack character; we do as well. That's why we are tempted to get angry when God is calling us to give grace. That's why we're tempted to beat our children with words when we are called to bless them with wisdom. That's why we are tempted to motivate our children with guilt, rather than igniting in them the courage of the gospel. That's why we take personally what really isn't personal at all and make it all about us. That's why there are moments when we are walking down the hallway toward one of our children's rooms and we're actually angry because one of our children has the audacity at that moment to need parenting!

Much of our struggle as parents is rooted in the fact that God is still working, with the zeal of transforming grace, to mold new character into our hearts. Without that grace we would be left to the coldness of our hearts and the dysfunction it would create in every dimension of our lives. When you confess that when it comes to character struggles, you are more like your children than unlike them, then you deal with situations when character problems are revealed with patience, kindness, and grace. This confession frees you to see these moments not as anger-producing irritants, but as what they are: moments of grace. God has set every element of these situations up to reveal the hearts of your children to you. He has manufactured this moment to remind you again that the heart of your child is not operating the way that he intended. And he has done this because he loves your child and he wants you to be an instrument of insight, confession, and change in your child's heart.

When you begin to think this way, rather than being mad that you have to deal with this stuff all the time, you will be blown away at the magnitude and zeal of God's grace. How could it be that God could love your children this much? How could it be that he could care so much about what is in their individual hearts? How could it be that he would exercise his sovereign power in such a specific way as to make sure that the lack of character in the hearts of your kids would be exposed in such clear ways? But he does care and he does rule situations in our families, not so that they would be comfortable, but so that they would be something better, something restorative. Because God is a God of incalculable grace and boundless love, we will have character opportunities with our children. God will give them to us again and again. The question is, Will we recognize them and deal with them with patient wisdom and restorative grace?

A Stunning Connection

The Bible makes a connection to the source of character issues that makes these issues profoundly more important to the task of parenting than you would otherwise think they are. Character problems are more than relational hassles or situational irritants. They are more than what causes horizontal disharmony in our lives. There is something deeply moral and theological about these problems, and only a person who takes the Bible seriously would ever come to understand this. Why do all of our children (and us too) tend to be impatient, unkind, demanding, and complaining? Why do they tend to fight with each other, say things that are unkind, and lack in functional love? Why do they want to be first in line, be the center of attention, and find it easier to be served rather than serve? Why do they tend to look for ways to avoid work, shift the blame, and think that they know more than they actually know? Why do they tend to argue for argument's sake, be more competitive than is necessary, and think they're the one always getting the short end of the stick? Why do they not act lovingly toward people they say they love, why do they not like to share, and why do they tend to excuse rather than confess? Why?

If you do not understand the source of character issues, it's hard to handle those issues in a way that leads to recognition, confession, and change. This is where the connection that Scripture makes is as practical as it is brilliant. When I came to understand this connection, it fundamentally altered forever the way I looked at my children (and myself) and the way that I dealt with their character problems.

I want to examine Romans 1 with you because this is where this stunning character connection is made for us. The verses below break into God's discussion of what sin does to the function of every heart of every person who was ever born. That means it describes to you the hearts of your children.

> . . . because they exchanged the truth about God for a lie and worshiped and served the creature rather than the Creator, who is blessed forever! Amen. . . .
>
> And since they did not see fit to acknowledge God, God gave them up to a debased mind to do what ought not to be done. They were filled with all manner of unrighteousness, evil, covetousness, malice. They are full of envy, murder, strife, deceit, maliciousness. They are gossips, slanderers, haters of God, insolent, haughty, boastful, inventors of evil, disobedient to parents, foolish, faithless, heartless, ruthless. Though they know God's righteous decree that those who practice such things deserve to die, they not only do them but give approval to those who practice them. (Rom. 1:25, 28–32)

I don't know if you caught it as you read the passage above, but the Bible connects character issues to the most significant of all human functions—worship. What this passage is telling you as a parent is that the heart of your child always lives under the rule of someone or something. And what rules the heart of your child will shape and determine how he deals with the situations and relationships of everyday life. This passage also alerts you to the fact that this means that there is a daily war that is being fought on the turf of the hearts of your children. It's a war for control. Will the heart of your child be controlled by love for the Creator (worship) or by craving something in the creation (idolatry)? Further, it lets you know that it's only when your heart is ruled by the Creator that you will respond as he has designed you to respond to the circumstances and people in your life. Think of how this helps us understand, untangle, and intervene in situations like what I described to you in the beginning of this chapter.

So we'll start with this question: On the Tuesday in our story, what's ruling the hearts of those children? The answer is easy: pleasure. Is pleasure an evil thing? No, it's not. God placed us in a pleasurable world and created us with an ability to enjoy its pleasures, but pleasure must not rule your heart. If the desire for pleasure controls your heart, you will not respond appropriately to the situations and people in your life. So because these children were getting what they wanted, they didn't care about what their mother was going through. If pleasure controls your heart, you won't love and serve the people in your life as God has called you to.

It's not wrong to want a little control over your life, but if the heart of your child is ruled by control, he will fight your authority every time. It's not wrong for your child to want to be right, but if a desire to be right rules his heart, he will be endlessly argumentative. It's not wrong for your daughter to want to be accepted, but if human acceptance rules her heart, she will be tempted to do things she shouldn't do to get it. It's not wrong for your son to enjoy material possessions, but if the desire for things rules his heart, he will be constantly dissatisfied and demanding. It's not wrong for your children to want a little independence, but if independence rules their hearts, they will fight you every time you try to exercise a bit of parental control over them. The character issues in the lives of your children exist not just because they want bad things, but because they become enslaved to good things. You see, a desire for even a good thing really does become a bad thing when it becomes a ruling thing.

The biblical connection of character issues to worship is incredibly helpful as you think about how to understand and respond to those issues in the lives of your kids. And you have to understand your parental job description in these moments. Your children don't understand the connection that the Bible makes between character and worship. If you would go into the family room and ask, "Why didn't you offer to help Mommy? You could see she needed help," your children wouldn't answer, "Because there's idolatry in our hearts. Rather than our hearts being ruled by God, they were ruled by pleasure, so we didn't really care about what you were going through. Come on, Mom, you know that misplaced worship always leads to character deficiency." Your children will never say that because they don't understand why they do the things they do. Parents, that's your job. It's your God-given job to unfold deep mysteries of the universe to your children. To make connections for them that are not only insight-giving, but life-transforming as well. They need you to do more than announce failure, instill guilt, attach a consequence, and walk away. If you can't have a conversation that makes these important heart/worship connections, schedule it later. But capture these opportunities. These moments are moments of grace. God is revealing to you what your children don't see and don't understand so you can show it to them so that the Spirit of God can work concern, conviction, and confession into their hearts.

Every exposure of the heart is a grace. Every conversation is a blessing. How amazing is God's love that he would ever care about one moment in one family in one house somewhere on earth, and he would work so that hearts would be exposed, truth spoken, and rescue provided. If he did that only once, it would be an incredible miracle of grace, but he does it again and again in millions of homes every day. That he cares for us and our children is too magnificent for our little human brains to fully grasp. When you have to deal with a situation that has been made difficult because your child lacks character, you are not being cursed, you're being graced. God turns these moments of failure into moments of redemption and asks you to participate in his gracious rescue agenda.

When your teenage daughter, Sally, comes home at the end of her school day and says, "Everybody in my class is going up to that old abandoned camp for the weekend to hang out and have a sleepover," you say, "Do they have permission to be there?" She says a bit impatiently, "Mom, it's an abandoned camp; there's no one to give permission." You then say, "Will there be adult supervision?" Sally says, "Come on, Mom, we're a bunch of young adults. We're capable of an overnight at an old camp. What do you think is going to happen?" So you respond as calmly as you can, "Sally, I'm not comfortable with you going somewhere for the weekend without permission to be there and without adult supervision." Sally says, "But, Mom, everyone is going. I will be the only one that can't. How embarrassing is that? I wish you weren't so hung up. I wish you would trust me for once. I can't believe I have to go to school tomorrow and tell my friends that my mom won't let me go!" You say, "Sally, I wish I could say yes, but I just don't think it's a good plan." Sally walks away while saying, "I knew you'd say no; you always say no."

The problem with Sally in this situation is not that she has broken a rule. You had never given her the "no weekends at abandoned camps" rule. The problem with Sally is that she lacks character and that lack of character has put her at odds with you. Now, think back on the connection that has been the focus of this chapter. What's ruling Sally's heart right now? Sally doesn't understand it, but the big motivating factor in her heart is what the Bible calls "fear of man." Sally craves being in the "in crowd." She craves being accepted by her peers. She fears being rejected. All of this is understandable and normal, but dangerous as well. The Bible says that fear of man is a snare (Prov. 29:25). You see, it is natural to want to be accepted because God has designed us to be social beings, but if human acceptance is where Sally looks to get her identity and inner sense of well-being, then she will be tempted to do and say things that she should not in order to get it.

Because fear of man rules Sally's heart, she is angry that her mom is concerned, rather than being thankful for her love. But Sally doesn't understand why she's feeling what she's feeling and doing what she's doing because she doesn't understand the connection between character and worship. Sally needs something more than a parent who will say a firm *no*; Sally needs a parent who will help Sally understand what's in her heart and how it shapes the way she responds to her mom. These are not the hard moments of parenting; these are wonderful moments where eye-opening and heart-changing conversations are given an opportunity to happen.

A Descriptive List

Go back and look at Romans 1:28–32 again. Notice the connection between worship ("since they did not see fit to acknowledge God") and character (the poor character list that follows). If you examine this list, it describes quite clearly the things we deal with with our children every day.

> *Envy.* How often do you have to deal with the conflict that results because one sibling is jealous of another?
> *Strife.* Is there ever a day when you don't have to deal with some kind of problem between your children?
> *Deceit.* How often are our children less-than-honest about what they have said or done?
> *Gossip.* Do you not find your children being regularly seduced by the temptation to talk negatively about someone to someone else?
> *Insolent.* To be insolent is to be rude and unmannerly. What parent doesn't have to deal with this on a regular basis?
> *Haughty.* It's the pride in the hearts of our children that again and again makes parenting them difficult.

Boastful. Boastfulness is pride with an open mouth. Our children are way too comfortable with announcing that they are better, smarter, prettier, faster, stronger, more likeable, etc.

Foolish. There is never a day when somehow, someway you are not confronted with the foolishness of one of your children.

Heartless. It is sad to see how heartless our children can be in their responses to one another.

Not only does this list capture the things that you are required to grapple with daily as you parent your children, it also tells you why you have to deal with them. Your children don't so much need *character management* as they need *worship realignment.* They don't first have a character problem; they have a worship problem that produces a character problem. Because of this they need more than character critique; they need to be given insight into the worship function of their hearts and how it shapes the way they react in the relationships and situations of their daily lives. They really do need truth that has the power to set them free.

Yes, it is true that our children are slaves to what they don't see, and because they are, they respond in ways that they don't understand. They need the grace of insight, the grace of wisdom, the grace of patient instruction, and the grace of daily forgiveness. And our ability to give this grace to our children starts by acknowledging that the list we have considered not only describes them but us as well. The worship of our hearts gets kidnapped, too, by something in the creation, and when it does, we don't respond as we should to the people and situations in our lives. Like our children, we need a patient Father who will help us to see our hearts so we can confess what is there and reach out for the change that only he can empower. Parents who are humbly willing to confess their need of parenting care don't resent those moments when they are called by their Father to give the same care to their children.

Think of how God works in your life. He is not content with just forgiving you for your sin; having forgiven you, he is zealously committed to transforming you. He doesn't just target those intentionally rebellious moments. He works on the character of your heart as well, so that you progressively become what he designed you to be. Because he is committed to character change, your Lord goes after the idols of your heart and he will not rest until every thought, desire, choice, word, and action is fully rooted in the worship of him. You and I are still blessed every day with his fatherly care because the war of worship still rages in our hearts.

Now God calls you to do with your children what he graciously does with you every day. Help your children understand and own what rules their hearts. Help them see how what controls their hearts shapes how they respond to people and situations. Make the character/worship connection again and again and again for them. And as you do, remember that you are functioning as a tool in the hands of One who has the willingness and power to free the hearts of your children from what has captured them, and in freeing them, implant new character in their hearts.

Bobby's Story

Bobby was a bit of a geek. He had a bulbous body, was not very coordinated, and was a bit socially awkward. Because of this Bobby hated school. There wasn't a day when Bobby wasn't made fun of. Bobby would beg his mom to stay home, and he would cry as he told her at the end of the day about how he was treated. But when Bobby was around ten or eleven years old, he discovered that he had a good sense of humor, and when he made jokes, people liked him. So the classroom became a place for Bobby to perform for acceptance. Bobby was good at it. Sometimes Bobby said something so hysterical that the teacher would have to turn her back to the class because she was laughing too. Bobby had become the typical disruptive class clown.

Then the notes started coming home about the distraction that Bobby created in his class, and Mom would talk to Bobby. Bobby would promise his mom that he would do better, but he didn't do better. Before long the administration of the school threatened Bobby with expulsion, and his dad lectured Bobby about what life would be like if he had no education, but nothing changed.

I met Bobby when he was thirty-five. He had asked to talk with me. The first time we met, I asked Bobby why he was there, and I'll never forget what he said: "I'm just so tired of playing the buffoon." Bobby had never finished his schooling; he had a string of short-term jobs and a series of broken relationships. He was a lonely, broken man. So I began to talk to Bobby about his heart. It's not wrong for Bobby to have wanted to be accepted. It's not wrong that Bobby hated the rejection that he faced every day. But if these things rule your heart, they will do damage to your life—and that is exactly what happened to Bobby.

I remember Bobby saying to me, "Paul, I'm thirty-five years old, and you're the first person who has ever talked to me about what rules my heart." Bobby wasn't saying this in a self-excusing way; he was just wondering aloud. Bobby was raised in a Christian home. He went to a pretty good church and attended a Christian school, but no one had ever talked to him about what we have considered in this chapter. No one had explained these liberating mysteries that the Bible reveals for us. No one had told him that no human being could ever give him the identity and rest of heart that he was looking for. No one helped him to understand that the failure in his life was rooted in hooking his heart to something that would never deliver.

Bobby is now an owner of his own business. He's married and a father. Bobby is an elder in his church. I wrote this chapter because I am concerned about what will happen to the Bobbys that are being raised by Christian parents about the world. Will our Bobbys learn early what controls their hearts and how what controls their hearts shapes the character of their lives? Or will our Bobbys continue to respond to people and situations in ways they don't understand out of hearts that are progressively captured by what can never deliver what they seek? Will their parents fail to see moments of character deficiency as moments of grace? Will their parents fail to make connections that have the power to change their hearts? Will we bring the gospel of liberating, transforming grace to our Bobbys in little moments of everyday life? What will happen to our Bobbys?

11

false gods

Principle: You are parenting a worshiper, so it's important to remember that what rules your child's heart will control his behavior.

I WANT TO DEEPEN and expand the conversation about worship because this issue may be the most important thing every parent needs to understand about the children that God has called them to parent. I want to start our examination of the truth that you are parenting worshipers with a series of questions and two illustrations.

Every parent needs to ask three questions:

1. Why do my children do the things they do? Every parent goes through those moments when they're confused, surprised, or dismayed by the choices, words, and actions of their children. Why does your little boy resist your instruction or guidance? Why do your kids have such difficulty getting along with one another? Why is your daughter so obsessive about her appearance? Why is getting in the car such a source of sibling war-making?

2. How does change take place in children's hearts and lives? If you see your child doing things that are selfish, wrong, rebellious, foolish, or destructive, you will long to see them change. Sadly, because most Christian parents can't answer the first question, they can't answer this one either. Therefore they reduce their parenting to trying to control their kids' behavior, rather than working every day to be a tool of change in God's hands.

3. How can I be a tool of change in the hearts and lives of my children? It is vital to understand that God has called you to something deeper than to manage, guide, and control your child's behavior. God has called you to be an agent of his rescuing, forgiving, transforming, and delivering grace. You cannot allow yourself to settle for anything less.

Why have I started with these three questions? Because the answer to these questions is found in a single word: *worship.* Every single thing your child has ever said or done is rooted in worship. There is no more foundational observation about human beings than the one we are now examining. There is no such thing as a little boy or little girl who does not worship. There is no such thing as a middle-schooler or teenager that does not worship. Worship is not only the shaping force of our children's behavior, but it is the explanation of the choices they make and the actions they take. Without understanding the expansive implications of this truth about your children, you will be deep in the woods without a GPS.

Children do what they do because of what they worship. Because of this, change is not so much about behavior management, but worship realignment. Being an instrument of change means getting at worship issues with your child. You may be saying to yourself right now, "Paul, I don't have any idea of what you're talking about. I just want my kids to eat what they're told, to go to bed when they're told, do their homework, and stop fighting with one another. What you're writing about seems more theological than practical." I do understand that reaction. I've heard it from many parents as I've tried to get them to understand the significance of this truth. So let me give two parenting illustrations.

You decide to take your son to Toys"R"Us. (Don't go there, the Devil is in that place!) You have been there before, and you know all the temptations that will greet your son. So you put him in the cart, and you go down the center of the aisle so his little arms can't reach all the things he would like to grab and take home. You eventually get to that final checkout aisle, which is designed to be a conspiracy against your parenting. Located in that narrow aisle are those $6.95/$7.95 blister-wrapped items. They are deliberately positioned right where your son can see them and touch them. So your son says, "Mommy, I want one of those." You say, "Johnny, Mommy is not going to buy you anything else." Johnny immediately says, "But Mommy, it's a Captain X Bongo figure and I don't have any of those." You say a little more sternly, "Johnny, Mommy has said that she is not going to buy you anything else." "But Mommy," Johnny whines, "Billy has all of them. He even has the play station. I'm the only boy I know that has to go to someone else's house to even hold a Bongo figure. Mommy, if you get this for me, I promise I will never ever ask for anything again." Now, with a bit of frustration in your voice, you say, "Johnny, Mommy is not going to buy you anything else. Mommy bought you a puzzle, and that's all you're going to get today." At that point, Johnny begins to scream as if you had physically hurt him. It is very embarrassing; you can feel all the people around you staring at you. It's one of those moments when you wish you had a button you could press that would open a trapdoor to an underground tube to your house. You just want to get out of there as fast as possible.

Now, if your interpretation of the embarrassing public skirmish with your son is that it was just another nasty encounter between you and him, you don't know your child and what makes him tick. Yes, the tension in the moment is horizontal (parent to child), but what has caused it is vertical (your child and God). Understanding this is essential to understanding the task that God has called you to. You see, Johnny wants something more than just a mom who will provide for him. In fact, although he doesn't know it, Johnny wants something more than a God who will provide for him. Read carefully what I am about to say. What little Johnny actually wants is to be that God. He wants to be the one who stands in the center of his world and rules it. He wants to think and it will happen. He wants to speak and it will be done. He wants what he wants, when he wants it. He doesn't ever want to be told no. He doesn't want anyone to stand in his way. Why? Because Johnny instinctively puts himself in God's position. He instinctively makes life all about him.

It would be bad enough and difficult enough if Johnny just had a problem with submitting to human authority, but he has a profoundly more significant problem than that. Johnny has a problem with his mom's authority because he has a problem with God's authority. He has a problem with his position as a son because he wants God's position. The nasty moment in the toy store is about something way more significant than a little boy's desire for another toy. It is about the deeper cravings of his heart, and if you do not understand that, you will not help him.

Your sixteen-year-old daughter spends what you think is a ridiculous amount of time in the bathroom every morning. She never seems to have enough clothes. She devours fashion magazines and websites. You have begun to think that she must be the selfie queen of her generation. She not only constantly takes selfies, but she also takes selfies in the mirror, so she has selfies of her taking selfies! You are concerned that she puts on too much makeup and wants to dress too provocatively.

You are saddened that what she looks like on the outside gets way more attention and concern than what is happening on the inside. As you listen to her talk, you are concerned with how important the reactions of friends (particularly boys) are to her and her appearance. She's constantly telling you that she thinks she's ugly or fat. She tells you she hates her nose, thinks her calves are too big, and wishes she wasn't so flat-chested. With all her attention on her appearance, she frets every time she goes out and seldom seems happy for very long.

It's not hard to step back, examine, and understand what's going on here. This teenager's problem is way deeper than just the fact that she is vain (and she is). It is way deeper than the fact that she is materialistic. It is way deeper than the fact that she spends too much time and money on her appearance. It's way more significant than the fact that she cares too much about the opinion of others. It's way deeper than the fact that she has bought into the surrounding culture's view of beauty. It's bigger than the fact that she is not committed to modesty. All of these things exist in this girl because something at a deeper level is broken, and change will only ever take place in her life if you get at that deeper thing.

All these things are operating in this girl's life because of worship. That's where the brokenness exists. You won't solve the problem by limiting the time she has in the bathroom, putting her on a strict clothing budget, requiring her to quit complaining, taking away her fashion magazines, or okaying her outfits before she leaves the house. If that's all you do, the minute she is out from under your control, she will go back to the old appearance-obsessed way of living.

What is going on in this teenage girl's life is profoundly spiritual. It is about the deepest commitments and cravings of the heart. It is about where she looks for life, for satisfaction and contentment, for identity and belonging, for meaning and purpose, and for her inner peace and security. It's about where she looks to find hope and strength. It's about what gets her up and helps her face another day. It's about what is her functional God. The sad thing is that she has attached her identity and the security of her heart to something that can and will not deliver. In her lack of heart rest, she becomes all the more addicted and obsessed. She focuses more and works harder to be beautiful, attractive to her friends, and alluring to the boys around her. She desperately needs parents who will do more than try to control her choices and behavior. She needs parents who understand her at heart level and are working to be instruments of heart change. What is raging in her life is a war of worship, and sadly, there is a good possibility that her Christian parents don't know that.

What Is Worship?

Worship is a tricky word for most of us, because when we think of worship we tend to think of formal religion. When most people think of worship, they think of Sunday morning, a gathering of fellow believers for singing, offering, and preaching. But worship is not just a religious function; it is a human function. Worship is something everyone does every day. You don't have to know you are worshiping to be worshiping. Because everything in our lives is shaped by worship, there is a way in which everything that we do is somehow, some way, an act of worship. You can't divide life into moments that are times of worship and moments that aren't.

Worship is that inner desire for wonder, amazement, and awe that every human being possesses. It is that craving to be fulfilled. It is that constant search for life. It is wanting personal meaning and purpose. It's the drive to look to someone or something to give you identity. It's that universal hunger for inner peace. It's that life-long hunt for God. It's the fact that we always live in service of something or that we always live in control of something. It's the reality that no one is godless. We all give our hearts to the one true God or to some created God replacement. Read the powerful things Scripture has to say about the worship/idolatry of our hearts and the hearts of our children.

> "You shall have no other gods before me." (Ex. 20:3)

> "Love the LORD your God with all your heart and with all your soul and with all your might." (Deut. 6:5)

> "Take care lest your heart be deceived, and you turn aside and serve other gods and worship them." (Deut. 11:16)

"The LORD your God will circumcise your heart and the heart of your offspring, so that you will love the LORD your God with all your heart and with all your soul, that you may live." (Deut. 30:6)

"And do not turn aside after empty things that cannot profit or deliver, for they are empty." (1 Sam. 12:21)

"How long shall my honor be turned into shame? How long will you love vain words and seek after lies?" (Ps. 4:2)

"For all the gods of the nations are idols, but the LORD made the heavens." (Ps. 96:5)

"Their idols . . . have mouths, but do not speak;
    eyes, but do not see.
They have ears, but do not hear;
    noses, but do not smell.
They have hands, but do not feel;
    feet, but do not walk;
    and they do not make a sound in their throat.
Those who make them become like them;
    so do all who trust them." (Ps. 115:4–8)

"I am the Lord, that is my name;
    my glory I give to no other,
    nor my praise to carved idols." (Isa. 42:8)

"Thus says the LORD, the King of Israel
    and his Redeemer, the LORD of hosts:
'I am the first and I am the last;
    besides me there is no god.'" (Isa. 44:6)

"Therefore speak to them and say to them, Thus says the Lord GOD: Any one of the house of Israel who takes his idols into his heart and sets the stumbling block of his iniquity before his face, and yet comes to the prophet, I the LORD will answer him as he comes with the multitude of his idols." (Ezek. 14:4)

"Therefore, beloved, flee from idolatry." (1 Cor. 10:14)

"Do not love the world or the things in the world. If anyone loves the world, the love of the Father is not in him." (1 John 2:15)

"And the world is passing away along with its desires, but whoever does the will of God abides forever." (1 John 2:17)

I have pulled out just a few passages of hundreds in the Bible. Why is this such a strong biblical theme? Because the God who created us knows that everything in our lives and the lives of our children is driven by worship. He knows that whether we are conscious of it or not, every day of our lives is a war of worship.

These uniquely human inner cravings—for life, for peace, for identity, for hope, and for meaning—that are at the heart of what worship is, were intended to lead us to our Creator, to seek the help that only he can give and to give our lives in service of him. But sin causes all of us to exchange worship and service of the Creator for worship and service of the creation. The position that God was to have in our lives gets functionally occupied by something in the creation. The catalog of things we worship is as wide as the catalog of things that God created. So from the earliest moments of your child's life he or she will worship something. I don't mean intentionally or self-consciously, but your children will give their hearts to something. Their words and actions will be shaped by the rule of something. If your child looks for identity in material possessions, they will be all too focused on physical things and materialistic in their approach to life. If they look to people to give them life, they will be a slave to the opinions of others and work too hard to please them. If they look to get their inner sense of well-being from being in control, they will resist your authority as a parent and want to write their own rules. If they put themselves in God's position, they will be entitled, demanding, complaining, needlessly competitive, and proud.

All the dysfunction, disobedience, disrespect, and resistance in the lives of your children, which distress you and make parenting hard, have worship roots. All of the willingness, compliance, respect, responsibility, honor, peacemaking, and good choices, which cause you to celebrate, are rooted in worship too. Knowing this is foundational to doing what God has called you to do as you parent your children.

The capacity of the heart of our children to worship is meant to drive them to God. You can't allow yourself to separate your parenting from this truth. Your parenting must be shaped by the most radical thing that anyone could ever say about your children. Your kids were made for God. They weren't just made for a good education, a good job, a good house, a good marriage, and good citizenship. These things have value, but they are not the reason your children have been given life and breath, and they must not be our ultimate goals as parents. Our children were made to find life, hope, identity, and meaning in God. They were made to surrender their will and their natural gifts to him. They were created to stay willingly inside God's boundaries. Many parents unwittingly separate Christianity from everyday life as they parent their children, and in separating Christianity from daily life, they fail to make worship as important as it is. Yes, they want their children to believe in God, to go to church, and to do what is right, but the primary focus of their parental energy is on producing children who are mannerly, do well at school, and succeed in sports and music. So they try to control all of the behaviors that will get in the way of these goals. Because of this they do not focus on the heart and what rules the heart. And because they fail to think about the heart, they miss those wonderful moments of grace where God is revealing the heart of the child so that his parents can be God's tools of rescue, leading our children to insight, confession, and repentance. They are left with trying to get their children to do what is right without addressing the heart, failing to understand that if they could do that, Jesus wouldn't have had to invade earth on his mission of rescue.

The capacity of your children to worship is the most important biblical insight for parents. What captures your attention with your children? The fact that they fight so much, that they tend to work harder at getting out of work than doing work, how they're doing at school, the circle of friends they crave to be accepted by, the sexual insanity and temptation that seem to greet your children every day, the chaotic look of their rooms, the fact that they tend to be girl-friend and boyfriend focused, that they argue over things that seem so unimportant, their materialism, how much time they spend on their cell phones, their Facebook/selfie view of life, their horrible diet, the amount of time extracurricular activities distract them, or their lack of spiritual interest? Of course, everything I have listed is important because the list captures where your children live everyday and what captures their interest and controls their time. But it's important to understand that these things do not cause your children to be what they are and to do what they do. No, these are the locations where what is really important to them, that is, what functionally rules their hearts, are revealed.

As a parent you have to look through the lens of the truth that your children are worshipers in order to understand and deal with all that is going on in your children's lives. God will use the normal stuff of daily responsibilities, opportunities, relationships, and temptations to expose to you what is going on in the heart of the worshipers that have been entrusted to your care. He will do this again and again, because he is a God of gloriously zealous and patient grace. He is after the heart of your child even when you don't have the sight or the sense to be. And he will be faithful to give you opportunities to see and help your children to see the God-replacements that are progressively gaining control of their thoughts, desires, feelings, choices, hopes, dreams, cravings, values, and goals. He is on a mission of rescue, and he has appointed you to be his representative on-site in the lives of your children. For a parent, there is no biblical observation, no parental job description, and no daily goal more important than what we are talking about right now. As one of my favorite theologians, Bob Dylan, sings, "You gotta serve somebody."

Since your children are worshipers, you must be committed to being an instrument of seeing. Since sin tends to blind your children to their own hearts, because sin is deceitful, you must look every day for opportunities to be an instrument of seeing in their lives. It's not enough to announce rules and enforce punishment. It's not enough to get out your portable pulpit and give another lecture. It's not enough to strategize how to protect your child from himself. All of these things have a place, but they are not enough. You see, if you see wrong in the hearts of your children, but they don't acknowledge that wrong, they will resist your help and they will not commit themselves to change. Here's how it works. Your children cannot grieve what they do not see, they cannot honestly confess what they do not grieve, and they cannot repent of what they haven't confessed. Read what was prophesied of Jesus: "And I will lead the blind in a way that they do not know, in paths that they have not known I will guide them. I will turn the darkness before them into light, the rough places into level ground. These are the things I will do, and I do not forsake them" (Isa. 42:16).

When you work to help your children to see and own what is motivating them to want what they want and to do what they do, you are doing the work of the Messiah, Jesus, who sent you. Parenting is not just about getting your children to do something, but helping them to see so that they would desire to do it. Every day you are working to give them light—light that illumines the heart and allows them to confess what is there. It's important to understand that your children resist your help because in their blindness they do not think they need it. Sight-giving is an irreplaceable step to lasting change in the lives of your children. You must always ask, "What right now does God want my child to see that he is not now seeing and how can I help him see it?" Maybe there is no more important question than this one.

Since your children are worshipers, a vital skill for you is to learn how to lead them to confession. It is so tempting to confess for your children: "This is what you did! This is why you did it! And this is what you're going to get!" It is so tempting to make threats: "You don't ever want me to see you do that again!" It is so tempting to instill guilt: "I just can't believe that you would do this to me!" It is so tempting to call names: "Sometimes you're such a brat!" It's so tempting to condemn: "Sometimes I wonder if you'll ever make anything of yourself!" It's so tempting to compare one of your children to another: "I can't understand why you can't just do what is right like your sister; you've been raised in the same home!"

It's so tempting to raise your voice, to make your vocabulary more pointed, to shake your finger, to get up in the faces of your children and, sadly, to slap their faces, to shove, push, pull, or pinch. None of these things opens up the hearts of your children. None of them gives them eyes to see. None of them gives them a voice to confess. All of these things shut the hearts of your children down. These things make your children angry and defensive. They make them want to escape you rather than hear you. They take the focus away from their own hearts and on to you. They put you in the way of what the Messiah is doing in the hearts and lives of your children, rather than make you a tool of it.

Leading your children to confession is about having tender, patient, understanding, and insight-giving conversations with your children that are intended to get them to examine what they haven't acknowledged and to begin to accept responsibility for the thoughts, desires, and choices that cause them to do what they do. Leading your child to confession is not about being a prosecutor, leading them to sentencing and judgment. It's not about building a case for indictment. It's about wanting your children to experience the rescuing and transforming power of grace. It's not "Do this and you'll get this" parenting. It's "You need help, and I'm here to help you" parenting. So you commit yourself to asking this question day after day after day: "Where is God calling my children to own responsibility for their thoughts, desires, choices, and actions, without excuse or shifting the blame, and how can I help them do it?"

To say your children are worshipers means you have no power to free them from their biggest problem. We can teach our children, we can warn our children, we can work to protect our children, we can guide our children, we can be examples to our children, we can discipline our children, we can correct our children, but we have no ability at all to deliver our children from the natural idolatry of their hearts. Admitting our inability is not giving up as a parent. On the contrary, this humble admission is the soil in which effective, Christ-centered, grace-driven, hope-infused, and heart-changing parenting grows. If you confess your inability, then you do not allow yourself to think that a louder voice, more graphic vocabulary, or a bigger threat is going to alter the worship content of your child's heart. What our children need is the rescue of divine insight, divine conviction, and a divine commitment to change. Without this they will say to themselves that they are okay and that they don't need your parental help or the heavenly Father's.

Because your children are worshipers, your only hope for them is the grace of the Lord Jesus Christ. This point directly follows the previous. If there is no human parental help that is powerful enough to rescue our children from their own hearts, then there is only one place where help is to be found. It is in the person and work of the Lord Jesus Christ. Now clearly, this doesn't mean that we do nothing. It means that all that we do, we do with the desire to be sharp tools in his powerful hands. We faithfully hold God's high standard before our children, we lovingly confront their wrong choices and actions, we work to help give them insight into their hearts, we are humbly honest about our own heart struggles, we talk to them again and again about the grace to be found in Christ Jesus, and we model his patience and forgiveness. We do all these things again and again because we believe the Savior is in us, with us, and for us, and we believe he is for our children because he has graciously placed them in a family of faith.

We are more like our children than unlike them. This final point is essential. If you are going to be God's tool in your children's life, you have to require yourself to remember that their worship struggles are your worship struggles as well. Like them, you exchange love for God for some craving for something in the creation. Like them, you let good things become bad things in your heart because they become ruling things. And like them, you tend to be blind to what's in your heart. So, the rescue that your children need, you need as well.

When you admit this, you stop being self-righteously judgmental and start being compassionate. You stop saying things like, "When I was your age, I would have never thought of doing such a thing." Or, "I just can't believe that you would think of doing what you do." Or, "I just don't know where this stuff comes from." You see, it really is true and worth repeating that no one gives grace better and more willingly than a person who has admitted that he desperately needs it himself. How about bringing that humble, grace-thankful heart to all that you do with your children?

Parenting is being willing to expend your time, gifts, energies, and resources in a daily battle of worship as God's tool in the lives of your children. It's never just about food, friends, Facebook, homework, sleep-time, clothes, household rules, or sibling squabbles. Those things are struggles because there is a deeper war going on inside the hearts of your children. Every struggle in these areas is an opportunity that is given to you by a God of amazing grace to get at those deeper issues for the sake of the redemption, rescue, and transformation of your children. And God will give you everything you need to engage yourself in that deeper war.

Control

Principle: The goal of parenting is not control of behavior, but rather heart and life change.

EVERY SEPTEMBER a sad thing happens. Thousands of supposedly Christian students go off to residential universities and begin the process of forsaking the faith.

Sharon has devised a good behavior award system. Every time her children have a good day, she puts a quarter in a very visible glass jar in the kitchen. When the jar is full, they get to go to McDonald's for their favorite dinner.

Jim's sons shared the largest bedroom in their suburban home, but they just couldn't seem to get along with one another. Jim solved the problem by getting a $100,000 loan and building an addition on his home so his now teenage sons would each have a room of their own.

Becky created the concept of "Saturday Silent Suppers" so that at least one day a week she could enjoy dinner with her husband

and their four boys without it descending into noisy chaos. The boys now dread the Saturday dinner meal because they have to eat in total silence.

Fran and Joe have put a monetary value on every chore that they want their children to do. On her iPad, Fran has created a chart that keeps track of the chores each child has completed and how much money each has accumulated as a result.

Bill has created a quiet place in the house where his children are required to go and sit by themselves when they have been disrespectful or disobedient. He says he not only wants them to sit and think about what they have done, but to dread being told to go into that room.

Sam sent his son to college with no money to spend. If he needs or desires anything, he has to call home, and Sam puts that amount into his ATM account. Sam not only wants to teach his son to be thrifty, but to carefully control his spending.

All the Smith children have cell phones, but they're on a pay-as-you-go plan so that their parents can easily control the amount of time they spend on their phones.

When her children were still in elementary school, Mary came up with the idea of "Good Grade Gifts." A monetary value was attached to each good grade, and when the child had earned twenty dollars, she could go to her favorite shop or web store and make a purchase.

Jenny got so tired of her children fighting over the remote control for the flat-screen that she created a "Remote Control Usage" chart to schedule who had the remote when and to finally create a little family room peace.

Jared can't wait to be old enough to get out from under his parents' control and their endless rules and make a few decisions of his own.

Liz hates the way her mom makes her dress and often changes clothes after she has left the house.

Cindy is exhausted at the end of another day of trying to do anything she can to control her little gang of three boys and one girl.

One theme is woven through each of these vignettes. Did you see it? These are parents from different places, with children of a variety of ages, yet each parent has given himself or herself to the same thing. Not everything they're attempting is wrong, but it's all inadequate. Each little slice of parenting life that I've given you above pictures either an attempt by a parent to control the behavior of a child or the results of those attempts. Do our children need to be controlled? Absolutely! Is controlling the behavior of your children enough of a goal as a parent? Absolutely not!

In this chapter I want to pick up and expand a theme of this book: as a parent you have been called to something more foundational than the control of the behavior of the children that God has entrusted to your care. I have touched on that subject in many of the chapters you have already read, but I want us together to focus our attention on this subject more fully here.

What Our Children Need

Consider this: the true needs of your children are what form your job description as a parent. What you do as a parent shouldn't be shaped by the values of the surrounding culture. What you do as a parent shouldn't be shaped by your reaction to how you were parented. What you do as a parent shouldn't be shaped by what you have dreamed your children could become. What you do with your children should not be shaped by the ups and downs of your emotions. Your parenting of your children should be shaped by what God says every human being needs. What follows is a list of those foundational human needs, but here's what I want you to notice about the list: not only are these the things that are to shape your parenting, but these are the things God promises and does for each of his children. What God as your heavenly Father knows you need, he has called you to provide as you represent him in the lives of your children.

These are things that every parent should be daily committed to lovingly, patiently, and faithfully deliver to their children. These are more fundamentally important than many of the things that command our attention, eat up our schedules, and sap our energies as parents. If God promises these things to you, he knows you need them, and you cannot independently provide for them yourself. And if that is true of you, it is also true of your children, so God calls us to be the delivery agents of these good things in the lives of our children.

God does call you to exercise daily control over your children, so that you regularly provide these things for them. You must give them God's law and the household rules that apply those laws to daily living. You must constantly teach them what is right and how to live right. You must step in again and again and protect your kids from themselves. You must prepare them to live well in this broken world. You must structure their days and teach them how to invest in their future. You must impart wisdom to them and teach them what it looks like to live it out. You must confront them when they do what is wrong. You must discipline them in the face of their rebellion. To do these things you must be in control and you must exercise faithful control over your children. But even if you faithfully did all these things, you would not have done enough.

Confused? Well, read carefully through the list of needs and accompanying passages that follows.

Guidance

- "Where there is no guidance a people falls, but in an abundance of counselors there is safety." (Prov. 11:14)
- "For you are my rock and fortress; and for your name's sake you lead and guide me." (Ps. 31:3)

Protection

- "Like the birds hovering, so the LORD of hosts will protect Jerusalem; he will protect and deliver it; he will spare and rescue it." (Isa. 31:5)
- "He who dwells in the shelter of the Most High will abide in the shadow of the Almighty." (Ps. 91:1)

Instruction

- "Good and upright is the LORD; therefore he instructs sinners in the way." (Ps. 25:8)
- "Thus says the LORD of hosts. . . . Will you not receive instruction and listen to my words? declares the LORD." (Jer. 35:13)

Wisdom

- "If any of you lacks wisdom, let him ask God, who gives generously to all without reproach, and it will be given him." (James 1:5)
- "And because of him you are in Christ, who became to us wisdom from God. . . ." (1 Cor. 1:30)

Authority

- "Let every person be subject to the governing authorities. For there is no authority except from God, and those that exist have been instituted by God." (Rom. 13:1)
- "And Jesus came and said to them, 'All authority in heaven and on earth has been given to me.'" (Matt. 28:18)

Rules

- "The law of the LORD is perfect, reviving the soul; the testimony of the LORD is sure, making wise the simple." (Ps. 19:7)
- "But you are near, O LORD, and all your commandments are true." (Ps. 119:151)

Structure

- "For I know the plans I have for you, declares the LORD, plans for welfare and not for evil, to give you a future and a hope." (Jer. 29:11)

- "The counsel of the LORD stands forever, the plans of his heart to all generations." (Ps. 33:11)

Preparation

- "The heart of a man plans his way, but the LORD establishes his steps." (Prov. 16:9)
- "His divine power has granted to us all things that pertain to life and godliness." (2 Pet. 1:3)

Understanding

- "I have more understanding than all my teachers, for your testimonies are my meditation." (Ps. 119:99)
- "The unfolding of your words gives light; it imparts understanding to the simple." (Ps. 119:130)

Confrontation

- "He who disciplines the nations, does he not rebuke? He who teaches man knowledge. . . ." (Ps. 94:10)
- "But exhort one another every day, as long as it is called 'today,' that none of you may be hardened by the deceitfulness of sin." (Heb. 3:13)

Discipline

- "Know then in your heart, as a man disciplines his son, the LORD your God disciplines you." (Deut. 8:5)
- "For the Lord disciplines the one he loves, and chastises every son whom he receives." (Heb. 12:6)

Warning

- "He said to them, 'Take to heart all the words by which I am warning you today, that you may command them to your children, that they may be careful to do all the words of this law.'" (Deut. 32:46)
- "Moreover, by them is your servant warned; in keeping them there is great reward." (Ps. 19:11)

Love

- "The LORD, a God merciful and gracious, slow to anger, and abounding in steadfast love." (Ex. 34:6)
- "For God so loved the world that he gave his only Son. . . ." (John 3:16)

Forgiveness

- "But with you there is forgiveness, that you may be feared." (Ps. 130:4)
- "As the Lord has forgiven you, so you must also forgive." (Col. 3:13)

Security

- "He gives them security, and they are supported, and his eyes are upon their ways." (Job 24:23)
- "You, O LORD, will keep them; you will guard us from this generation forever." (Ps. 12:7)

Read back through this list and ask yourself what's missing. True, it's a wonderful list of things everyone needs, and if you make sure that your kids have these things, well, that's a very good thing. But it is an incomplete list. God promises you all of these things, but as your heavenly Father, he would not be satisfied if you had them all. Exercising control over your children so that you deliver these things, and in so doing shape their behavior, is not enough. God, who called you to the task, promises you more and has called you to more. In fact, the need that your kids have for these things is rooted in a much deeper, more foundational need. God calls you to do more than just battle for control. He calls you to engage in a battle that is the battle of battles. It is the battle that is the main drama of the story of redemption that is the main theme of his Word. He calls you to keep this battlefront in the center. He calls you to understand that all the other good and needed things that you work to provide for your children aren't the goal of your parenting, but a means to a greater end. He calls you to be as zealously committed as he is to this deeper need, so that you do not get distracted and sidetracked, becoming satisfied with a job partially done.

He has called you to the job of jobs, and he will be with you and provide for you every single thing you need. He calls you to exercise faithful control, but never to be satisfied with the fact that you have. Your dear children desperately need your parental control, but they will not be all God has designed them to be if that's all that you give them.

Every Child's Deeper Need

If you carefully watch your children and stop to think about the things that you have to deal with as their parent, you will be driven to the conclusion that they need more than careful parental control because something has gone wrong inside them. It's not just that they make foolish choices, or argue with you endlessly, or mistreat one another, or are entitled and demanding, or act as if they have wisdom that they don't, or question your authority, or find "no" more natural to say than "yes," or seem scarily attracted to the world, or seem to lack interest in the things of the Lord, or pout when they don't get their way, or refuse to be happy until they get what they want. It's that all these things are moment-by-moment symptoms of a deep, abiding, and inescapable need that they came into the world with. And no matter how successfully you control their choices and behavior, your control cannot and will not free them from this deeper need.

To properly understand this need and the shaping impact it must have on your parenting, there is no better place to look than Psalm 51.

> Have mercy on me, O God,
>   according to your steadfast love;
> according to your abundant mercy
>   blot out my transgressions.

Wash me thoroughly from my iniquity,
and cleanse me from my sin!

For I know my transgressions,
and my sin is ever before me.
Against you, you only, have I sinned
and done what is evil in your sight,
so that you may be justified in your words
and blameless in your judgment.
Behold, I was brought forth in iniquity,
and in sin did my mother conceive me.
Behold, you delight in truth in the inward being,
and you teach me wisdom in the secret heart.

Purge me with hyssop, and I shall be clean;
wash me, and I shall be whiter than snow.
Let me hear joy and gladness;
let the bones that you have broken rejoice.

Hide your face from my sins,
and blot out all my iniquities.
Create in me a clean heart, O God,
and renew a right spirit within me.
Cast me not away from your presence,
and take not your Holy Spirit from me.
Restore to me the joy of your salvation,
and uphold me with a willing spirit.

Then I will teach transgressors your ways,
and sinners will return to you.
Deliver me from bloodguiltiness, O God,
O God of my salvation,
and my tongue will sing aloud of your righteousness.
O Lord, open my lips,
and my mouth will declare your praise.
For you will not delight in sacrifice, or I would give it;
you will not be pleased with a burnt offering.

The sacrifices of God are a broken spirit;
  a broken and contrite heart, O God, you will not despise.

Do good to Zion in your good pleasure;
  build up the walls of Jerusalem;
then will you delight in right sacrifices,
  in burnt offerings and whole burnt offerings;
  then bulls will be offered on your altar.

There is so much help in this psalm for understanding the deepest need of your children that I think you could write a whole parenting book from it alone. The implications of what David confesses and cries out for set a whole new agenda for what God has called us to in the lives of our children. As I explore the implications of this psalm for understanding the task of parenting, I want you to notice the focus of David's confession. He doesn't say, "I messed up and I'm sorry." Far from it. David is deeply aware that he has more than a behavior problem. When you read Psalm 51, you are hit with the fact that embedded in David's confession of specific and concrete sins is a cry for God's help with a even deeper moral drama. Let me draw six agenda-setting observations from this psalm for your work as a parent.

1. Your Children Need to See Their Sin, So They'll Cry Out for God's Mercy

Psalm 51 begins with a cry every human being should make, but sadly billions don't. You only make this cry when you have come to the point where you acknowledge that the greatest danger in your life lives inside you not outside you, and because of that you are a person in desperate need of God's help and the helpers he has placed in your life. There is no more important function for a parent than this: to lovingly and patiently bring our children to the point where they too cry out for God's mercy. Crying out for God's mercy happens only when you have acknowledged the sin that is inside you from which you are not able to free yourself. Children who begin to humbly and willingly acknowledge their sin not only run to God for his help, but they quit resisting the help, guidance, correction, and instruction of their parents too. How sad would it be if you successfully managed and controlled the behavior of your son or daughter, but they left your home never acknowledging the sin in their hearts and their desperate need for God's mercy?

What if our kids received a good education and landed a good job, and are healthy, successful, and well-liked, but have no sin awareness and no hunger for mercy? Perhaps David's cry for mercy confronts us that as Christian parents, our problem isn't that we set the parenting bar too high, asking too much of our children. I think we set the bar too low, settling for horizontal success, when God has called us to be agents of radical heart and life change.

2. Your Children Need to Understand the Nature of Sin, So They Don't Minimize Its Danger (vv. 1–3)

Here is something you need to consider. It is not negative and condemning to talk to your children about their sin. Think of it this way: all loving parents warn their children about the dangers around them that they need to be aware of and avoid. You do this because you love your kids and you want to protect them from things that could harm them. There is no more harmful thing in a child's life than his own sin. To be made aware of it and its power to destroy is a good and loving thing.

It's important to understand that your children don't come into the world seeing their sin or acknowledging its gravity. That's your job as a parent. Here again, Psalm 51 is incredibly helpful because the three words that David uses for *sin* graphically portray its life-crushing danger. The most basic word that David uses for this deep brokenness of heart is *sin*. Sin means that your children, with all of their natural gifts, abilities, and efforts, will consistently fall below God's standard. To use the bow-and-arrow illustration, it's not that your children aim and miss God's mark. It's that they aim, pull back on the bow, and shoot—and every single arrow falls short of the target. Not one arrow even hits the outer ring of the target. Every arrow falls to the ground short of God's targeted destination. Sin means our children, on their own, have no ability to live as God has ordained and commanded them to live. No parental control, no educational system, no personal success will give them this ability. They need divine intervention.

The second word that David uses is *iniquity*. Iniquity is moral uncleanness. It is heart-breaking to consider, but biblically true, that our children come into this world unclean on the inside. What does this mean? Moral uncleanness means that they are naturally attracted to what God says is wrong, and because they are, they are susceptible to the myriad of temptations that greet them every day. The problem with our children is deeper than the fact that they have less-than-perfect parents, or siblings that are selfish, or friends that are mean, or that they live in a world that is broken. Their problem is that they come to all of these situations with a susceptibility to temptation and an attraction to what is wrong. If you look carefully, you will see this attraction and susceptibility operating in your children almost every day.

The last word that David uses to describe sin is *transgression*. It's not just that sin makes our children unable, and it's not just that sin makes our children susceptible. Sin causes our children to be rebels. Transgression means to consciously and willingly cross God's boundaries. It is seeing the "No Parking" sign and parking there anyway. It is seeing the "No Trespassing" sign and climbing the fence and going in anyway. As I wrote earlier, it may be hard to accept, but our children are natural rebels against authority (God's and ours), and they have a natural inclination to want to step beyond the boundaries that have been set for them. They will tend to inch closer and closer to the line, finally crossing it in an attempt to experience the temporary feeling of being self-governing. The struggle with our children is not just that they are ignorant and in need of instruction. If all that our kids needed was good instruction in order to live as God designed, then, I repeat, the life, death, and resurrection of Jesus wouldn't have been necessary. They need that divine intervention because, by nature, they are rebels against any authority but their own. You see that in the little girl who finds it easier to say no to her mommy than yes, or in the teenager who tends to argue every time he is told to do something, no matter what it is.

If your children are going to come to the place where they fear the sin that is inside them and seek God's help and yours, they will need to understand the gravity of sin. These three words capture the danger of sin and how important it is for your children to acknowledge that it lives inside their hearts.

3. Your Children Need to Understand That Their Problem Is Not with Their Parents, but with God (v. 4)

It seems almost weird for a man who has committed adultery and murder to say that his sin is against God and God alone. But the fact that David says this means he understands not only the gravity of what he has done, but the seriousness of the condition of his heart that caused him to do it. Our children need to understand this too. Every sin is vertical. Every sin is a fist in the face of God. Every sin is a desire to remove God from his throne and sit there yourself. Every time your children sin, they tell themselves that they are smarter than God, that they know better and can write their own rules. Every sin is claiming independence from God. Every sin puts your children in the center of the world and makes life all about them.

You see, our children were created to live for God, to give their lives to him, to willingly stay inside his boundaries, and to do what they do for his glory. Sin is about refusing to live for the glory of another. It's about your sons or daughters reducing their life down to their wants, their feelings, and their happiness. No sin is purely horizontal. When your children are disrespectful to you, they dishonor God, because it is God who has commanded them to respect their parents. When your children fight with one another, they are fighting against God, because it is God that called them to live at peace with one another. When a teenage boy gets a girl pregnant, his moral violation is against God, who commands him not to use the body of another for his selfish pleasure.

As a parent, you must always remember the verticality of the wrong that your children do and not make it just about you. But you must also help them to understand that they were made for God, created to do his will, and because this is so, every wrong thing they do is done against him.

4. Your Children Need to Understand That Sin Is a Nature Problem That Produces Behavior Problems (v. 5)

When David says, "Behold, I was brought forth in iniquity, and in sin did my mother conceive me," he is saying that my biggest problem is not situational, it's not geographical, it's not relational. No, it's my nature. I was born a sinner. I came into the world this way. This point is significant and vital for you and your children to understand. It's not enough to say that your children sin. You and they must come to recognize that they *are* sinners. Sin is not first a bad behavior; sin is a condition that produces bad behavior. A sinner can't simply say to himself, "Tomorrow I am not going to sin anymore," and actually pull it off.

It is loving to help your children to understand that it's not enough to confess that they sometimes do what is wrong. They need to come to the place where they confess that wrong lives inside them, and because of that they are in desperate need of God's rescuing, forgiving, transforming, and delivering mercy.

5. Your Children Need to Understand That Since Sin Is a Heart Problem, the Only Solution Is a New Heart (v. 10)

You know when anyone cries out for a new heart that he has come to understand what sin, their greatest need, is all about. The only solution to the heart-infecting disease of sin that is in our children is a divine heart transplant. That's why Jesus was willing to come and subject himself to this fallen world, that's why he was willing to endure the cruelty of the cross, and that's why he had to exit his tomb, so that he could deliver to us and our children the one thing we all need: a new heart. More than just being managed, our children need to be delivered. More than being instructed, our children need divine surgery. And it's not enough for you to recognize that need; they must come to recognize it as well, or they will continue to resist your help and not admit their need of God's.

6. Your Children Need to Be Taught to Run to the Only Place of Hope: The Forgiving Grace of God (v. 14)

I have written this elsewhere, but it needs to be said here as well: the doorway to hope is hopelessness. Until your children begin to give up on themselves, their wisdom, their strength, and their righteousness, they will not cry out for God's mercy. As long as they retain hope that they can make it without your help or God's, they will deny the sin inside them and take life into their own hands. The person who is seeking forgiveness is acknowledging that they are not in charge, that their life does not belong to them, that they have transgressed God's boundaries, and that they have no ability to buy their way back into God's favor. Then in their hopelessness, they run to the only place of hope: the forgiving and restoring hands of the Redeemer.

Parenting is about being used of God to bring your children to that wholesome and heart-changing place of personal hopelessness. This is not a process of condemnation, but of patient and loving rescue. Don't you want this rescue for your children?

You are called to make use of every opportunity that God will give you to help your children to become aware of the grave danger of the sin that lives inside them. You don't do this with irritation or impatience, but with grace, acknowledging that you are just like them, a person in need of God's mercy. Self-righteously pointing out the sin of others never works; it is offensive and condescending, and it will close down the hearts of your children. Ask God to give you the grace to come to them to talk to them about their sin as a person who is much more grieved by the sin that is inside you than the sin that is in them. When you come this way, your tenderness and humility becomes a workroom for God to do in the heart of your child what you can't do.

13

rest

Principle: It is only rest in God's presence and grace that will make you a joyful and patient parent.

IF YOU ARE STRUGGLING to be patient, finding it hard to be joyful, and sometimes dreading the next day of parenting, could it be that your struggle to be tender and loving toward your children is rooted in the reality that you are overburdened and overwhelmed? Could it be that in your attempt to be a tool of grace in the lives of your children, you have lost sight of the amazing resources of grace that are the gift of the Father to all of his children? Perhaps in all your work to be used of God to produce children who know what it means to rest in his wisdom and grace, you have forgotten how to rest yourself.

As I fly around the world to lead parenting conferences, I meet exhausted and discouraged parents all the time. In fact, many of them have confessed to me that they dreaded coming to another parenting conference because they thought they'd be told again all the things they're not doing and leave the weekend feeling defeated and guilty. I've had mom after mom confess to me that they were at the end of their rope. I've had fathers ask me what to do about their anger. I've had parent after parent say that they know that they're doing and saying things that they know they shouldn't do, but they don't know how to stop.

Lydia said, "I start out the day telling myself that I'll do better, but by the end of the day, I'm screaming at them again."

Jason said, "I just hear my teenage son begin with his excuses and I get angry."

Marge said, "I have read all the good parenting books, but none of them have helped me."

Sue said, "How could it be that a three-year-old boy could have the power to make me so crazy?"

Ginny said, "I go to bed exhausted, I wake up exhausted. I don't have a lot of joy."

Frank said, "We got away last weekend because both of us were at the end of our rope with our four boys."

Sam said, "We were so excited about having children, but the excitement is long gone."

Sharon said, "I feel all the time that I just don't have what it takes to do all the things you're supposed to do as a parent."

Judy said, "I feel all the time that I just need to rest, but there is no rest for a parent."

Overburdened, overwhelmed, exhausted, and discouraged. I think this is the state of many more Christian parents than we think. And in our exhaustion and discouragement we are all too susceptible to doing and saying things that are not only unhelpful to our children, but that add to the burden of inadequacy we are already carrying. Occasionally we reflect on what we've been doing, and we're saddened that we've become what we determined we would not become and we've done what we told ourselves we would never do.

Here near the end of this book I want to give you good news. My prayer is that this news will not only lift your burden, but will clarify and simplify what God has called you to as a parent. God will never ask you to deny the reality of your everyday, moment-by-moment parenting struggle. He will never ask you to minimize how hard it is to raise up God-fearing, God-loving, God-serving children in this terribly broken world. He will never ask you to act as if you're doing well, when you're not doing well. He will never call you to rationalize away your children's rebellion and the struggle you have dealing with it in the right way. Biblical faith never requires you to deny reality; rather, it calls you to look at all the troubling realities in your life through the lens of the awesome glory and grace of your Redeemer. And as a parent, it's vital for you to understand that you only properly understand your daily troubles and struggles accurately when you look at them remembering the grandeur of the One who appointed you to the task.

You see, if you humbly face the reality of what your children need and how you struggle as a parent, but you do not remember the incalculable glory of the God who sent you, you'll soon feel overwhelmed, defeated, and guilty. As a Christian parent, you must not deny reality, but if you spend your mental and spiritual time meditating on the struggle and not meditating on your Lord, you're probably going down. When we're God-forgetful, we tend to load burdens on our shoulders that we cannot bear. We tend to give way to worry and fear, and we tend to get weakened by guilt. Perhaps the best thing that you do for your children is not something you do with them, but something that you do for yourself. Here it is: the most important thing you do for your children is to remember the One who sent you, and in remembering the One who sent you, teach your heart to rest. Bringing unrest to your parenting of your children never goes anywhere good. Vertical remembrance and rest is the soil in which the wholesome, good, and change-producing parenting grows.

It's so easy in the middle of any day of parenting multiple children to lose your mind. I don't mean that you've actually gone crazy. What I mean is that in the middle of all the busyness and confusion, without knowing it, you've forgotten who you are, you've forgotten who God is, and you've forgotten what you've been given. And because you've forgotten, you're shouldering burdens that you were never meant to carry and you're defeated by your inadequacy. I remember sitting on my bed in my dark bedroom late one night after having had a horrible conversation with my son where I had lost it and said all the things that I told myself I wouldn't say. In the dark, I felt so defeated, so alone, and so overwhelmed. I remember mumbling to myself and to my Lord, "I just can't do this anymore. It's just too hard." In that moment it hit me that God hadn't called me to do what I could not do all by myself. Yes, as a parent, he had called me to do things that were way beyond my natural abilities, character, wisdom, strength, and gifts, but he had never sent me out to do them *alone*. Aloneness is a cruel lie that will defeat us every time.

So I want to help you to remember and in remembering to rest. It is a heart at rest that will enable you to do the good things that God has called every parent to do.

The Best Parenting Passage in the Entire Bible

If I were to ask you what is the best, most practical, most helpful parenting passage in all the Bible, what would you answer? Most biblically literate Christian parents would answer, "Ephesians 6:1–4." That is a wonderfully helpful passage, but I want to take you to one that is even more fundamental. I think my choice will surprise you. And I think I know why.

You probably don't need me to tell you this, but I will: Your Bible is not arranged by topic. I know that frustrates some of you. You kind of wish it were arranged by topic, with little tabs on the end of the page that would direct you to your topic of need or interest. Well, the Bible isn't arranged that way. It's not arranged as it is because God made a massive editorial error. The Bible is arranged the way it's arranged because of wise divine intention. Your Bible is essentially a grand redemptive story. Maybe it would be more accurate to say that your Bible is a carefully theologically annotated story. It's a redemptive story with God's essential explanatory notes.

This means you can't approach your Bible topically and get the best that it has to offer you, because the Bible wasn't designed to operate that way. For example, if all you do to understand parenting is go to the passages that have that word in them or seem to address that topic, you will miss the majority of the information the Bible has for you as a parent. Rather, your Bible works this way: to the degree that every passage tells you something about God, something about yourself, something about the disaster of sin, something about life in this fallen world, something about what God has called you to, and something about the operation of grace, to that degree every passage tells you about every area of your life. That's how your Bible works.

So I want to take you to a passage that almost is never mentioned in the context of parenting, but has in it everything you need to know and understand in order to experience the rest and courage of heart that fuels good, godly, perseverant parenting.

I want to take you to one of the final, and surely the best known, of Jesus's commands to his disciples. This passage is popularly known as the Great Commission, and because of that has been most often applied to the formal evangelistic mission of the church. But I am deeply persuaded that its call is much wider than that and because it is, it offers real hope and help to every Christian parent. It captures with clarity what God has called you to and what he has promised you as you take on this hugely important and life-long task. As we near the end of this book, I thought it would be helpful to consider its implications and encouragements.

> And Jesus came and said to them, "All authority in heaven and on earth has been given to me. Go therefore and make disciples of all nations, baptizing them in the name of the Father and of the Son and of the Holy Spirit, teaching them to observe all that I have commanded you. And behold I am with you always, to the end of the age." (Matt. 28:18–20)

I cannot think of any directive from the mouth of Jesus that is a more appropriate call to every Christian parent than this one.

If someone were to ask you what the ultimate job of a parent is, what would you answer? Well, the answer is here. Your job is to do everything within your power, as an instrument in the hands of the Redeemer who has employed you, to woo, encourage, call, and train your children to willingly and joyfully live as disciples of the Lord Jesus Christ. This is more important than how they do in school, or how positively they contribute to the reputation of your family, or how well they set themselves up for a future career, or how well they do in sports and the arts, or how well they are liked by adults and peers.

These things aren't unimportant, but we must not let them rise to the importance of this one thing. Your children must come to learn early that their lives don't belong to them. They must understand early that they have been given life and breath for the purpose of serving the glory of another. They must learn that they do not have the right to follow their own rules or write their own laws. They must surrender to the fact that their lives are meant to be shaped, not by what they want, but by what God has chosen. They need to know early that they are worshipers whose capacity to worship is meant to be owned by the One who created them with this capacity.

Here's the core mission of parents: to raise up children who approach everything in their lives as the disciples of Jesus. Now, let's be honest here; this way of living is not natural for anyone. It's natural for our children (and us) to live as if they are the owners of their own lives. So they don't just need to learn that this is not true, but they need to admit their need of the grace of divine rescue, forgiveness, and empowerment. If you are going to raise willing disciples of Jesus, you need to patiently communicate the story of his amazing grace to your children again and again. You see, God's law has no power to turn your children into disciples, but his grace does. *Are you working to be used of God to make disciples of your children?*

This leads us to the second part of the call of Jesus. As a parent you are called to teach your children to observe everything that Jesus has commanded. It is awesome to think that God's will extends to every single area of your children's lives. He has a plan for their thoughts, their desires, their choices, their words, their decisions, their relationships, what they do with their bodies, what they do with their money, what they do with their worship, how they invest their time, how they conduct themselves in relationships, how they relate to authority, their relationship to the church, the way they steward their physical possessions, and what they allow to occupy their minds and capture their hearts.

Our children must learn to look at life through the lens of the will and plan of their Creator. What we are talking about is helping them to develop a comprehensive biblical worldview that is a way of looking at life that is distinctively God-centered and biblically driven. Not only is this not natural, but it is also important to remember that your children will be bombarded by the seductive and attractive voices of many other competing worldviews. They will be hit again and again with other ways of thinking about who they are and the purpose of life. They will be challenged by those who don't believe in God and who will tend to mock the faith of those who do.

It's not enough to tell your children what to do and what not to do. This passage calls every parent to a deeper goal. You must teach your children how to think about everything in a way that is pointedly God-centered. Now, if our children are ever going to think about themselves and life this way, they need to be willing to submit to the wisdom of someone greater. Let's again admit that this is not only not natural for our children, it's not natural for us. It's natural for our children to think that they are right and that they know what's best. It's natural for our children to resist recognizing and surrendering to a greater wisdom.

So once more, we are confronted with the fact that as parents, we have no power to turn our children into the thinking and living disciples of Jesus Christ. They will become his disciples only as they are rescued by his grace. As parents, we are called every day to faithfully participate in what is impossible for us to produce. And if sadly we fall into thinking that we have the power to produce it, we will invariably end up doing bad things. This is precisely where the promises of this passage are so encouraging. Perhaps you're thinking, "How can I get up every morning to do what is impossible to do and not end up exhausted and discouraged?" The rest of the passage answers that question.

Our passage makes it very clear that Jesus would not ever call you to this huge parenting task without also blessing you with his mind-blowing promises as well. If you understand and embrace his promises, then you can give yourself to participate in what is impossible for you to produce and not have discouraging or even paralyzing anxiety in your heart. In fact, good, loving, faithful, grace-driven parents only ever grow in the soil of a heart at rest. Jesus's promises are not so much promises, but reminders of the unshakable identity of every one of his children. The two promises here are meant to remind you of what the great heavenly Father has become for you by grace. These promises define for you not only who God is, but who you are as his child.

You see, your rest as a parent will never be found in the success of what you are doing or the success of what your children are doing, because there will always be some degree of struggle, weakness, and failure there. No, rest is found in the One who sent you and in what he wills always to do for each of the ones he sends to represent him. If you look horizontally for your rest, you will always end up disappointed. There will be days when you'll be able to see the fruit of your labors in the lives of your children, and there will be days when it seems like you have accomplished almost nothing. This is why the words we are about to consider are so important.

Jesus begins his commission not with calling us to something, but with comforting us with these words: "All authority in heaven and earth has been given to me." Wow! Just let your heart marinate in this truth. These words tell you that it is impossible to be in any situation, any location, any circumstance, and any relationship at any time that is not at that time being ruled by King Christ. Now let that color the way you think about parenting your children. There is never a moment, in any location, where you are in a situation with one of your children that is not under the wise, careful, and powerful control of the One who sent you into it. Yes, there will be moments when you will lose control and there will be moments that seem out of control, but there is never a parenting moment that exists outside the control of the King who sent you.

You can rest when you don't understand what is going on because the One who sent you is never confused and never surprised. You can rest in the middle of parenting mysteries because you know that the One that you represent knows no mystery. You can rest when your authority seems weak because you know that the One you serve has authority that can never be weakened or defeated. And here's why he is telling you this: he wants you to know that he is exercising his authority for the benefit and success of the mission to which he has called you. Your success as a parent does not rest on your shoulders but on his. The fruitfulness of your work as a parent does not rest on your authority but on his. Your Lord doesn't just call you to this huge parenting task; he also blesses you with the power, glory, and transformative ability of his unshakable rule. When your rule seems weak, you can rest in the reality that his rule on your behalf is never weak.

But that's not all. Jesus ends his call with these words: "And behold, I am with you always, to the end of the age." Stop reading right now and let yourself be amazed by these words. The Father, who sends you to extend his arms of fathering grace to your children, goes with you. He would never ever think of sending us out on our own. He would never coldly watch us at a distance as we go, work, and struggle. He would never sit idly by as we give ourselves to the single hardest, most comprehensive, most long-term, most exhausting, and most life-shaping task that a human being could ever take on. No, when your Father sends you, he goes with you.

This means that in every moment when you are parenting, you are being parented. In every moment when you are called to give grace, you are being given grace. In every moment when you are rescuing and protecting your children, you are being rescued and protected. In every moment when you feel alone, you are anything but alone because he goes wherever you go. It is impossible for your parenting to ever wander outside the light of his presence. He never forgets you, he never turns his back on you, he never wanders away for a moment, he never favors someone else over you, he never gets mad and refuses to be with you, he never grows cynical, he will never give up, and he will never ever quit. He is tenderly, patiently, faithfully, and eternally with you. You can bank on his care. You can rest in his presence.

So your hope as a parent is not found in your power, your wisdom, your character, your experience, or your success, but in this one thing alone: the presence of your Lord. The Creator, Savior, Almighty, Sovereign King is with you. Let your heart rest. You are not in this parenting drama alone. Your potential is greater than the size of your weaknesses, because the One who is without weakness is with you, and he does his best work through those who admit that they are weak but in weakness still heed his call.

The Great Commission summarizes your calling as parents, and its promises remind you of where you can look for help and hope. Let me suggest what hoping in the two redemptive realities (promises) of the Great Commission means practically for you in your everyday work with your children.

You will not be punished for your failure. You will fail as a parent. You won't always have the right reaction, you won't always say the right thing, and you won't always want what's best. It's important to remember that the One who sent you is not only your sender, he is your Savior, and his cross means you do not have to hide in shame and you do not have to be paralyzed by guilt, because Jesus paid the penalty for every moment when you fail as a parent. Since you do not have to fear God's anger in moments of failure, you can run to him for help and receive his forgiveness and help. Basking in the comfort of God's forgiveness then makes you able to own your weaknesses and confess them not only to God, but to your children as well.

You are welcomed by grace to new beginnings. Because your Savior is always with you, his grace is too. This means that you are free from living in the regret of things done wrong. He welcomes you to confess your failures and move on with the freedom and joy of his forgiveness. Embedded in his forgiveness is the promise of new beginnings. You see, he has taken away the burden of penalty for your sins so you can run to him, not only for his forgiveness but also for his help. In his help is the promise that you really can learn, change, and grow. His grace lets you put yesterday away and commit to new and better things today. The One who worked to forgive you now works to teach and mature you. Better parenting days ahead are made possible by his transforming grace.

You are not left to your limited resources. I know because I've been there: there are parenting days when it feels as if you have no wisdom and you've lost most of your strength. There are times when you don't know what to do. There are times when you know what to do, but it just doesn't feel that you have the inner will and outer strength to do it. Sometimes you feel exhausted before you begin the day, and sometimes you go to bed discouraged and not really looking forward to the next day. There are times when it feels that your kids have gotten the best of you or that you fell into doing something as a parent that you're not really proud of. In these moments when your weakness is all too evident, it is so important to know that God hasn't left you to the limits of your righteousness, wisdom, and strength. He knew exactly what this calling would demand of you, so he chose to be with you. Because he is with you, his power can enable you, his wisdom can direct you, and his character can restrain and redirect you. God knows what the ones he sends are made of, so he always works what only he is able to work, in them and through them. Your potential as a parent is hugely bigger than your independent personal resources.

God blesses you with the right here, right now wisdom of his Word. God has blessed you with the most amazing compendium of true wisdom, daily hope, and practical guidance for everyday living that you could ever want as a parent. Where is it found? In your Bible, his Word.

Now, to plumb the depths of his Word there is something that you need to consider. The Bible presents to you the grand explanatory story, the redemption story. This is the story that you need to know and understand in order to make sense out of your story as a parent and the stories of your children. By grace, God has embedded your personal story and the stories of your children in the larger story of redemption. And so you want to raise children who grow up thinking how they should think, desiring what they should desire, and doing what they should do because they always think of their identity and purpose from the perspective of God's story of redemption. Christian parenting is about raising children who live with a "God's story" mentality. Your God-given task is not just to raise children who know what God says is right and what he says is wrong, but who also are prepared to think and live biblically. Teaching your children to think in a way that is distinctively biblical is right at the center of what God has called you to. And so he has blessed you with the wonderful gift of his Word. Your Bible is not exhaustive, addressing everything in detail, or it would take an eighteen-wheeler to carry it to the Sunday worship service. But your Bible is comprehensive; it gives you wisdom to deal with everything you face in life. The best way to celebrate the gift of God's Word as a parent and to mine the depths of its wisdom is to take time to soak it in every day.

You do not have to load the burden of your children's welfare on your shoulders every morning. Every day remind yourself of this truth. The welfare of your children does not rest on your shoulders, but on the shoulders of the One who sent you. He has the power to do what you could never do. Unlike us he never is weak or weary. He never gets lost in his own discouragement or anger. Unlike us, he never looks back and regrets what he has done. He always does what is just, good, wise, kind, loving, gracious, and right. He loves our children more than we ever will—so much so that he died so that they would have everything that they need to be what they're supposed to be and live as they were created to live. Thankfully, the great heavenly Father's shoulders are big enough to carry what our small parenting shoulders could never bear, and he willingly bears the burdens that would otherwise crush and disable us.

God will never close his ears to your cries for help. Psalm 34:15 says, "The eyes of the LORD are toward the righteous and his ears toward their cry." First Peter 5:7 talks of "casting all your anxieties on him, because he cares for you." Jesus offered this invitation: "Come to me, all who labor and are heavy laden, and I will give you rest. Take my yoke upon you, and learn from me, for I am gentle and lowly in heart, and you will find rest for your souls. For my yoke is easy and my burden is light" (Matt. 11:28–30). Parenting is hard; it will expose your weaknesses and it will challenge your faith. There are times when you won't feel very good about what you just did or said. There will be days when your work with your children will seem more futile than helpful. But the good news of the gospel is that you don't have to hide your struggle. You don't have to act as if you're doing better than you are. No, you are welcomed by grace to cry out for help, you run to God in your need, and you are assured that not only will you not be turned away, but your heavenly Father will pay careful attention to your cries. "The LORD is near to the brokenhearted and saves the crushed in spirit" (Ps. 34:18).

Weakness is not a curse; it's a blessing. Because we all still tend to want to be independently strong, we tend to hate being weak. We hate feeling that we're not prepared. We don't like not knowing what to do next. We find it hard to acknowledge that we did it wrong. We tend to be afraid to confess that we're at the end of our rope. It is hard to be in the deep end of the pool and not be confident about your ability to swim. But for the children of God, weakness loses its terror, because the source of our rest is not our strength but the strength of our Father. It's liberating to be able to face your inadequacies without shame or panic, but that's just what the grace of God enables us to do.

But there's another thing. God will expose your weaknesses so that you will run to him, find his help in your time of need, and grow in your street-level confidence in his presence, power, and provision. Paul says it this way: "But he said to me, 'My grace is sufficient for you, for my power is made perfect in weakness.' Therefore I will boast all the more gladly of my weaknesses, so that the power of Christ may rest upon me" (2 Cor. 12:9). It's not your weaknesses that you should fear, but your delusions of strength. Delusions of independent strength are a curse because they tell you that you have power that you don't truly have and they keep you from resting and relying on the power that is yours in the presence and grace of the One who called you to be his representative in the lives of your children.

Success is about faithfulness, not results. You do not have to fear being judged by God for the results that you have produced. You are not manufacturing trophies; you are parenting children. As we have considered before, you have no power to transform your children from what they are to what they should be. No matter how righteously you act toward the children God has placed in your care, if they don't transact with God, they won't be what they're supposed to be and live as they were designed to live. You cannot make your children love, believe, surrender, respect, confess, forgive, serve, speak the truth, be pure of heart, and worship God. Only God can do these things. He would never call you to produce what you can't produce. No, he simply calls you to be faithful, to do good toward your children day after day after day, knowing that the results are in his infinitely powerful hands.

It really is true that good, godly, transformative parenting grows best in the soil of a heart at rest. Parent, is your heart at rest? Is your parenting fueled by trust? Or does worry haunt your heart? You have reason for rest. You have been sent, but the One who sent you rules every location and relationship he sends you to. You have been sent, but the One who sent you has packed up and come with you, so that you would have everything you need to do what he's called you to do. Fight the assessment that the job is too big. Fight the feeling that you are all alone. Meditate upon and celebrate his power and presence and go do what you've been chosen to do with courage and hope.

Principle: No parent gives mercy better than one who is convinced that he desperately needs it himself.

ONE OF THE BIGGEST ERRORS Christian parents can make is allowing themselves to forget. If you allow yourself to forget the daily mercies you receive from your Father's hands, mercies you could never earn, it will become easier for you not to parent your children with mercy. Mercy is tenderheartedness and compassion toward someone in need. Our children are just that—needy. They need guidance and protection, they need help and rescue, they need wisdom and instruction, they need confrontation and discipline, they need patience and grace, they need love and compassion, they need support and provision, and they need to see God and themselves with accuracy. There is not a day when your children do not need your mercy. Because of this, your primary calling as a parent is not first to represent God's judgment, but rather to constantly deliver his mercy.

You see, God's mercy is the need and hope of every human being whether they know it or not, and God's mercy is the place of comfort for every one of his children. Every day you are blessed with God's mercy. Check out these passages.

> "Surely goodness and mercy shall follow me all the days of my life, and I shall dwell in the house of the LORD forever." (Ps. 23:6)

> "Blessed be the LORD! For he has heard the voice of my pleas for mercy." (Ps. 28:6)

> "As for you, O LORD, you will not restrain your mercy from me; your steadfast love and your faithfulness will ever preserve me!" (Ps. 40:11)

> "Who redeems your life from the pit, who crowns you with steadfast love and mercy." (Ps. 103:4)

> "The LORD is good to all, and his mercy is over all that he has made." (Ps. 145:9)

> "Therefore the LORD waits to be gracious to you, and therefore he exalts himself to show mercy to you." (Isa. 30:18)

> "But God, being rich in mercy, because of the great love with which he loved us." (Eph. 2:4)

> "Let us then with confidence draw near to the throne of grace, that we may receive mercy and find grace to help in time of need." (Heb. 4:16)

These verses take us back to where this book began. Parenting is about being God's ambassadors in the lives of our children. It is about faithfully representing his message, his methods, and his character to our children. It's about working to make the invisible mercy of God visible as we respond with mercy toward our children. Hebrews 4:14–16 explains to us exactly what that looks like. Jesus was willing to subject himself to the hardships of life in this fallen world and be tempted in all the ways that we are, so that he would be an understanding high priest, able to sympathize with our weaknesses. The word that is used for *weaknesses* in verse 15 is used elsewhere in the Bible to refer to many different kinds of weakness. It really could be translated that Jesus is able to sympathize with the human condition or with our human frailty. Because he can sympathize with us, we can rest assured that he will bless us with mercy that is form-fitted for the need of the moment.

Parents, that's our model. Allow yourself to reflect on how much you need God's mercy now, reflect on how much you needed the mercy of your parents as you grew up, and let sympathy grow in your heart. Mercy is not about being wishy-washy. Mercy is not about letting down your standards. Mercy is not about acting as if the bad things your children do are okay. Mercy doesn't mean that you abandon discipline and correction. Mercy doesn't mean that you quit holding God's law before your children. Mercy is not letting your children decide what they are not mature enough to decide or control what they aren't able to control. Mercy is not about always saying yes and never saying no.

Mercy is parenting with a tender heart. Mercy is not taking your children's failures personally, but viewing their struggles with compassion. Mercy is about blessing your children with your patience. It's about being as careful to encourage as you are to rebuke. It's about discipline that is kind and correction that is gentle. Mercy is about being firm and unyielding and loving at the same time. It is about refusing to indulge your irritation and your anger. If you're parenting with mercy, you don't condemn your children with a barrage of harsh words. If you're parenting with mercy, you don't compare your righteousness to your children's sin, letting them know that their problem is that they're not like you. Mercy means not allowing your heart to grow bitter or cold. It is about always being ready to forgive, not making your children pay today for the sins of yesterday. Mercy is about moving toward your children with love even in those moments when they don't deserve your love. Mercy is about being willing to do things again and again without throwing it into your children's faces that you have to repeat yourself. It's about refusing to motivate your children by shame and threat. Here's what mercy means for your parenting: mercy means that every action, reaction, and response toward your children is tempered and shaped by tenderness, understanding, compassion, and love. Parenting is a life-long mission of humbly, joyfully, and willingly giving mercy.

Mercy Requires Mercy

I don't know about you, but mercy simply isn't natural for me. It's natural for me to be harsh. It's natural for me to be demanding and impatient. It's natural for me to be a bit irritated that I have to repeat myself. It's natural for me to be more upset by the wrongs of others than I am of my own. It's natural for me to want life to be easy and predictable and to be upset with those who get in the way of my plan. It's natural for me to find it more comfortable to have the people around me agree with me rather than debate me. I'm not always compassionate, and I don't always have a tender heart. I don't always respond with love and communicate with grace. I have to confess there are times when I am a pretty poor representative of God's mercy. And I am sure that I am not alone in my struggle. How well have you pictured God's mercy in the way you've responded to your children in the last month?

So I need help, and I suspect you do too. I don't need to be rescued from the sin, weakness, and failures of my children. I have been called to be a parent because of their sin, weakness, and failures. Every moment of the foolishness and failure of our children should remind us why the heavenly Father provided children with parents. My struggle is not them; it's inside of me. The fact that I struggle to graciously give what has been graciously given to me means that I still need to be rescued from me. Again, I am sure that I am not alone.

Since responding with mercy in the face of foolishness, immaturity, rebellion, and failure is not natural for us, the only hope for us as parents is that God would look on our failure as parents not with condemnation, but with mercy. His mercy toward us provides the only hope that we will have what we need to respond with mercy toward our children. And as we require ourselves to daily reflect on the mercy we are constantly receiving, need and gratitude soften our hearts and make us more ready and able to give to our children what we have received from our Father in heaven. You see, if you forget who you are and what you need, it becomes easier to parent your children without mercy. Think about how amazing God's plan is! God uses the needs of our children to expose how needy we are as their parents, so that we would do all that we do toward them with sympathetic and understanding hearts. God is working on you through your children, so that he can work through you for your children.

I remember the night very well. All day long my son had been particularly resistant. It felt that he was doing everything he could to make my day difficult. He argued and resisted and then denied that he had been argumentative or resistant. My well-planned day had been interrupted again and again by him. It was one of those days where parenting feels like a twelve-hour case study in futility. I grew more and more angry and resentful as the day went on, but I was unaware of it. Of course, he picked a fight with one of his siblings at the dinner table and turned supper into chaos. I couldn't wait for him to go to bed so I could have what was left of my day back.

Just when I was finally getting deep into what I was trying all day to do, I heard him upstairs. He wasn't asleep. No, he was arguing with his brother about something that made no difference at all. I jumped up from my chair and marched upstairs, more driven by the built-up frustration of the day than I realized. I went into his room and, without turning on the lights, let him have it. I angrily told him how he had trashed my day and that I wasn't going to have him trash my night. What I said to him was loud, accusatory, and personal. I let him know how much I did for him and how little he did for me. He lay in his bed and cried as I talked. I told him he better get to sleep— and quickly—or else, and I stomped out of the dark room in a huff.

As I walked down the hallway, I tried to justify my anger, but I couldn't. I tried to tell myself that he deserved what he got, but

I couldn't buy my own rationalization. I tried to reason that sometimes a tongue-lashing does a kid good, but it didn't work. And the reason it didn't work was that God immediately began to use that horrible parenting moment to expose what was in my heart. What I was experiencing was the painful blessing of the Spirit of God's conviction. I tried to go back to my work, but I was distracted by the guilt I was feeling. It was no use. I stopped doing what I was doing, and as I did, feelings of defeat washed over me. I couldn't believe that I had blown it again and this time in such a hurtful way. I couldn't believe that I had allowed myself to be controlled by what should never control me. I felt weak and unable. But as I felt those things, God was turning this very bad thing into a very good thing. That's what his mercy does. We learn that from the cross. The cross of Jesus Christ was the worst thing that ever happened (the killing of the Messiah) and the best thing that ever happened (penalty paid, sins forgiven) all at the same time.

God was letting me feel the shame, guilt, and pain of my outburst not as an act of condemnation but as a gift of mercy. I can say now that I am very thankful for that terrible night, not because I yelled at my son, but because of how God used that to expose my heart. That night I saw my need as a dad more clearly than I had ever seen. That night I was confronted with my irritability like never before. And that night I reached out for God's help in a way that was humble and new. By God's mercy, that night was a watershed moment. No, I didn't instantly change, but I was now aware of my weakness, and because I was, I began to cry out for God's help much more regularly. That night, God worked on me through my son so that he could work through me for my son.

How about stopping right now and confessing that you regularly lay down concrete evidence of your need for God's mercy as a parent? How about also celebrating that that mercy is yours as his child? And how about looking for ways to make the invisible mercy of God visible?

Responses of Mercy

Parents, here's what God has called you to: he has called you to be his first responders in the lives of your children. The fireman who willingly runs into a burning building or the EMT who runs up the stairs to assist a man who has just had a heart attack is on a mission of mercy. Being a first responder is always motivated by the combination of an awareness of need and compassionate desire to help. You are God's first responders, called to rush in with help when your child is in danger because of burning desire or an attack of temptation. That first responder is not there to lecture, judge, or condemn, but to provide the rescue that is needed but that the person cannot give to himself. First responders willingly expend their time and energy day after day on missions of mercy. God calls us as parents to live with the heart of a first responder, ready to run toward difficulty to provide, rescue, protect, help, and heal. You have not been called to be a bystander or a critic, but to be an agent of rescue. First responders don't take the needs of others personally, and they don't get mad that their day has been interrupted. They know what they are trained to do, and they are ready and willing to do it each time the need arises. So it is with us as parents; every day that you have with your children will provide you with another set of opportunities to go out on another mission of mercy. Every day you will be called into action to meet needs that your children can't meet on their own. Yes, parenting really is a lifelong mission of mercy, so let's consider what that looks like.

Look for every opportunity to shower your children with grace. Remember that the law of God has the power to expose the sin in your child's heart and the law is a wonderful guide for your child's living, but it has no power at all to rescue, transform, or deliver your child. As a parent you have to daily resist asking the law to do what only grace is able to produce. So you have not only been called to introduce the law to your children, but to be a constant model of God's grace in their life as well. Grant them the grace of compassion, the grace of tenderness, the grace of acceptance, the grace of loving wisdom, the grace of tender love, the grace of kind instruction, the grace of gentle discipline, the grace of perseverance, and the grace of fresh starts and new beginnings. And as you do these things, remember that grace is not about calling wrong right, because if wrong were right grace would not be needed. No, grace moves toward wrong, not to condemn, but to rescue, restore, help, and forgive.

Be careful to help your children see the heart behind the behavior. You must never forget that the mission of mercy you are on as you parent your children does not target just their behavior, but what forms and shapes their behavior: the heart. Anytime anyone is helped to see his heart, and in seeing his heart, to own his need, he is experiencing God's mercy. Asking your child what he was thinking and feeling, what he was wanting, or what he was seeking to accomplish gets him to examine his heart even for a brief moment. As you do this over and over again, day after day, your child grows in heart awareness. And his growing heart awareness gives the Holy Spirit an opportunity to work conviction into his heart and a desire for help and change.

Be patiently committed to process. You have to work to remind yourself that the mission of mercy you've been sent on by God is seldom an event and almost always an extended process. You won't have your first heart conversation with your son or daughter and have them say, "Mom, I get it. I have sin in my heart and my heart is ruled by things that shouldn't rule it and I need rescue and forgiveness. Where can I find the Redeemer?" That just won't happen. God has called you to a process of many mini-moments of insight that lead to many mini-moments of change. You must be patiently willing to have similar heart conversations again and again, praying each time that God would do in the heart of your son or daughter what you could never do.

Point your kids every day to Jesus. Because the only true hope and help for your child is found in the person, work, presence, and grace of the Redeemer, Jesus Christ, you must introduce your children to him early in their lives and look for opportunities every day to talk about his wisdom, power, sovereignty, love, and grace. Talk about why it was necessary for Jesus to live the life he lived, die the death he died, and rise again conquering death. Talk about how Jesus purchased their acceptance with God because they could never earn it on their own. Talk about how Jesus delivers them from sin, because they could never escape it on their own. Talk of how, if they come to him for help, he will never turn them away. Talk about how much you need the grace of Jesus every day.

Every time you discipline or correct your children, talk about their spiritual need and how it is met by the person and work of Jesus. Don't let a day go by without your children somehow, someway hearing the beautiful truths of the gospel of Jesus Christ once again. The mission of mercy you've been sent on as a parent has the gospel as its center. The gospel of Jesus Christ is the ultimate rescue mission.

Humbly accept your limits. You must daily resist the temptation that by the volume of your voice, by the strength of your words, by threat, guilt, or manipulation, by the power of your anger, by pointed finger and the stern look on your face, by elaborate or extended punishments, or by shaming and name-calling you can't do what only God can do. Faith as a parent means that you rest every day in God's presence and power, and because you do, you aren't frustrated by your limits. It is vital to remember that God will never ever ask you to be anything more than a tool in his powerful and capable hands. You are freed from the burden of changing your children. You have been liberated from the responsibility to make them believe. You have not been asked to cause them to think or desire what is right. You are simply called to expose what is bad, point to what is good, and talk about the Redeemer who can lead them from the one to the other. Resist loading onto your shoulders what your shoulders can't carry, and celebrate the fact that Jesus is with you, in you, and for you, doing through you what you couldn't do.

Remind your heart each morning to rest in the presence and power of your heavenly Father. For most parents worry is more natural than rest. It is more natural to once again work through your catalog of parenting "what ifs" than it is to trust God. It is more natural to dread what may happen than to believe that God is at work in your daily efforts. It's natural to envy another parent who seems to have it easier than you or whose kids seem to be doing better than yours. It's tempting to have a bad moment with one of your children and then catastrophize about what their life might become if they don't change. It's easy to have your parenting more driven by fear than it is by faith. So you need to start every day by reminding yourself of God's incalculable glory, his awesome power, his boundless love, and his amazing grace. And you need to tell yourself daily that God's glory doesn't just define him, but redefines who you are as his child. He has showered his glory down on you by grace. You need to start each parenting day remembering that all that God is, in his magnificent glory, he is for you by grace. Take a moment to remember and rest and then go out and parent with a heart filled with hope and courage, not because things are easy or going well, but because God is your Father, and he has unleashed his glory on you.

Willingly confess your faults. It is vital to remember that it's not just your children who are in that long process of change; you are too. You are not yet all that God's grace has the power to help you to be. You have not graduated from your daily need of God's rescue and forgiveness. Because of this, you will think bad things, you will desire wrong things, and you will give way to frustration, impatience, and anger. There will be moments when you lose your way. You will have a bad day. You will fall into saying and doing things more out of anger than grace. Good parenting is not just about being a good example; it is also about humbly confessing when you haven't.

If you've blown it, don't activate your inner lawyer and defend yourself; don't reason away your wrong and resist denying what you've done. You don't have to defend yourself, because Jesus has presented the ultimate defense to the Father in his life and death. So you are free to be humble, free to be honest, and welcome to confess without fear of God's rejection.

But your children need to hear your confession as well. It won't be long before they begin to understand that their mom or dad is less than perfect. They will be at the other end of your anger. They will feel the tension of your frustration. They will experience the pain of your harsh words. And if you talk all the time about their need to confess and seek forgiveness, but they never see you do the same, their frustration will grow and their hearts will be hardened. Humble confession turns wrong into a grace. It is a grace whenever your children see a humble heart modeled by you and as they do, it helps them to be more tender and willing to confess too.

Your children probably do not live under the delusion that you are perfect, and you better not give way to that delusion either. Encourage your children to seek God's help by being willing to show them how you seek God's help too.

Root all that you require, say, and do in the wonderful wisdom of Scripture. Your job as a parent is not to produce little clones who like what you like, dress like you dress, eat what you eat, enjoy the music you enjoy, share your aesthetic tastes, and are committed to your politics. Your job is be God's tool for the purpose of forming the image of God's Son in your children. And for that job, the Bible is your primary tool. Your goal is not only that your children would stay inside God's boundaries, but also that they would think about all of life from the perspective of God's Word. In the Bible your children learn who God is, who they are, and what the meaning and purpose of life is. They learn about the danger of sin and the rescue of God's grace, they learn how to fight temptation, and they learn what is right and what is wrong. In Scripture they are taught God's plan for their bodies, their minds, their relationships, their money and possessions, their sexuality, their relationship to authorities, and much more. But most of all they are confronted with the radical truth of a

God of glorious love who sent his Son to provide us rescue because we could not rescue ourselves.

Don't let Sunday or the children's or youth ministry be the only time your children are taught God's Word. Determine that how you relate to them, what you say to them, and the daily counsel that you give them will be driven and shaped by the truths of God's Word. Talk to them about how thankful you are for God's Word, how it not only has rescued you but also taught you to think about everything in a new way. Schedule a time every day to sit as a family and learn from God's Word and then talk about the truths of the Bible as your children are getting ready for their day, as you're providing transportation, as you're hanging out in the kitchen, and as they're on their way to bed (see Deut. 6:4–9, 20–25).

I'm not talking here about self-righteousness, quasi-angry biblical lectures used more to condemn than to rescue. I'm talking about your love for Scripture and the wisdom that you have gained from it naturally coloring your moment-by-moment interactions with your children. This is about you being a person of the Word so that you can grow up children who also love God's Word.

Don't treat opportunities like hassles. Here's the problem every parent faces: your best opportunities to get at issues of the heart in your children won't be on your schedule. They will come when you're in a moment you neither planned nor expected. There will be an argument in the car, a skirmish on the way to bed, a heated debate at the dinner table, an unexpected call from a teacher, the evidence of homework undone, something you've found in your children's room, a text that you discover on your child's phone, or a late-night refusal to obey. It is so easy in these moments to throw your hands up in frustration and say or do things that you shouldn't. So it's important to remember what has been a theme in this book. If your eyes ever see and your ears ever hear the sin, weakness, and failure of your children, it is never a hassle, never an interruption, never an accident; it is always grace. God loves your children and has put them in a family of faith, and he will reveal the need of their hearts to you so that you can be his tool of rescue and transformation. It is important to see these moments as opportunities of grace and resist turning a moment of ministry into a moment of anger.

Be slow to anger and quick to forgive. Perhaps there is no more important commitment in parenting than the commitment to own your anger and seek God's help to resist its draw. The things parents say and do in anger are invariably the things they live to regret. There are angry moments I wish I could take out of history and remove from the memory of my children. For parents, there is probably no more powerful argument for our need of grace than our struggle with irritation, frustration, and anger toward our kids. We need to seek God's help and to commit to resist. For some of us this means getting out of the room to calm down and pray, if only for a couple minutes. For some of us it means we are too angry to deal with something, so we will either wait until later or look for another opportunity. For some of us this means confessing when anger has gotten in the way of what God intended to do through us for our children.

Start every day by confessing the anger of the previous day and by asking God to give you the grace that you need so that your responses to your children would not be driven by the condemnation of anger, but by the rescue of forgiveness.

Pray before, during, and after. Parenting really is all about praying without ceasing from before your children are born to long, long after they leave your home. It is about constant prayer for God's grace for you and for them. It's quietly praying for them and you as they're getting up, as you're making them breakfast, as you're with them throughout the day, or as you send them off to school. Parenting is about praying for your children when you're helping them get an afternoon snack or as you're trying to get them to talk about their day. It's about praying for them as you instruct, correct, and discipline. It's about moments when your children hear you pray for them and hear you pray for you. Parenting is about teaching your children to pray.

You pray before, during, and after because prayer requires three things: a recognition of God's position, an admission of your need, and a surrender to God's plan. When it comes to parenting, you just can't pray enough. And the more you pray, the more you confess your limits, the more you rest in God's power, the more you'll be freed from the temptation to do in and for your children what only God can do.

Do all of these things over and over again. Parenting is about the willingness to live a life of long-term, intentional repetition. God has called you to a life of patient perseverance. He has called you to be willing to do the same thing over and over again. He's called you to slow down, settle in, and let him progressively do through you what only he can do. He's called you to believe that his plan and his timing are always right. He's called you to be willing to live with what is incomplete and to be thankful for each new step that is taken. And he's called you to look for opportunities every day to be part of his process of grace in the lives of your children. Here's the bottom line: he has called you not only to parent your children but to lay down your life for them. He has called you to expend the major effort, time, and energy of your life for your children's welfare. He's called you to be his tool of grace again and again and again. Parenting really is a life of holy repetition.

This book has been an elaborate discussion of one thing: God's call to you to be an essential part of his mission of rescue of the children he has given you. But it has not been just about the mission that he has sent you on, but also about the fact that he has gone with you. He doesn't ask you to do what you can't do, and he is eternally willing to do what only he can do. So he blesses you with his presence, power, wisdom, and grace. He faithfully parents you, so that by his faithful grace you can faithfully parent your children.

In every moment of parenting, the wise heavenly Father is working on everybody in the room. You are blessed to be chosen to go on the mission of missions, and you are blessed with his grace so that every day your parenting would be dyed with the most powerful force of change in the universe: mercy.

Study Questions

Introduction

Principle: Our children don't belong to us but to God. Parenting is about what God has planned to do in our children through us. As God's ambassadors, we must consider the big picture of what God is inviting us to be a part of as he works in the hearts and lives of our children.

1. What goals are you working for or building toward in your parenting? Describe how these goals sometimes get swallowed up into the daily grind of parenting.

2. In what ways does an "effective strategies" list fall short as you approach your task as parents?

3. Consider what it means to be given a new way of thinking about and responding to everything that comes your way in your role as a parent. Pray that the Lord would renew your vision, give you motivation and strength, and help your eyes to see the big, gospel picture of the task to which he has called you.

4. Why is your method of parenting in the repeated cycle of little unplanned moments so important?

5. Do you tend to approach parenting more often as an owner or as an ambassador? Which of the four areas that parents deal with (see pages

17–20) do you think will challenge you most as you consider God's invitation to be his ambassador?

Chapter 1: Calling

Principle: Nothing is more important in your life than being one of God's tools to form a human soul.

1. I gave three examples of things that compete to replace parenting as the highest treasure of our hearts: physical possessions, career success, and commitment to ministry. Which of these examples causes you to be less than faithful to your calling as a parent in the way you manage your time and energy?

2. Consider humbly and prayerfully asking your children and spouse for their perspectives on how you can make parenting a higher priority in your life (e.g., help with school work, be present for the bedtime routine, attend sporting events, play with your kids while your spouse makes dinner or goes shopping, etc.). What changes will you need to make in your career or ministry life to accomplish these things on a consistent basis?

3. Explain the importance of fostering God-consciousness and God-submission in your children. According to Deuteronomy 6:4–9, this is primarily the parents' responsibility. Are there ways in which you have allowed the church, government, or school to replace you in this task? If so, what will you do to reclaim your role and relegate these other entities to their proper supporting roles?

4. Deuteronomy 6 helps us see that we need to connect everything we require of our children to the story of redemption. How can you speak redemptively to your children even amid their failures and go beyond exercising your authority to point your children to God's grace?

5. Have you thought lately about the wonder of God's creation? Think of some ways you can point your children to the awe-inspiring work of

God in everyday life. Consider the makeup of an egg; the colors of fruits, vegetables, and flowers; the flight of a bird; the shape of a snowflake. Don't let a day go by without helping to open the eyes of your children to God's presence and glory.

Chapter 2: Grace

Principle: God never calls you to a task without giving you what you need to do it. He never sends you without going with you.

1. Have you ever thought of grace in terms of past grace, present grace, and future grace? What difference would it make in your day-to-day parenting if you understood and practiced present grace?

2. God doesn't call people to be parents because they are able. How is our inability and inadequacy part of God's good and perfect plan?

3. God never calls us to a task without giving us what we need to do it. Our parenting struggles are no surprise to God. What has he given to us that gives us hope and makes parenting possible? Will you commit to reminding yourself of this reality amid the difficulties?

4. How does seeing ourselves accurately as parents by God's grace change the way we approach our children?

5. Think about a recent unpleasant interaction with your child or children. What would you do differently after studying this chapter?

Chapter 3: Law

Principle: Your children need God's law, but you cannot ask the law to do what only grace can accomplish.

1. Before reading this chapter, what primary tool were you relying on to change the heart and life of your child? How did this shape the way

you were parenting in the formational, mundane, and not-so-mundane moments that shape who he or she will become?

2. What important part does the law play in raising our children? What is the law's weakness? How can you use the law for good in teaching your children?

3. In addition to teaching our children God's law, we are called to constantly exhibit and teach God's grace to them as well. Constantly. In everything we do. What are some of the opportunities in the life of your family in which you can begin to point your children to the presence and promises of God's grace?

4. In the midst of the stresses of life, do you sometimes find yourself wanting your children to just buck up, do what they're told, and behave in public? What would it take for you to long for much, much more than this?

5. I finish this chapter by reminding us of our role as ambassadors (see the introduction) and how we are called not only to preach grace, but also to live and model it for our children every day. This will no doubt require much humility and confession on our part. Consider some areas of sin that you may need to confess and admit your need for the Father's help.

Chapter 4: Inability

Principle: Recognizing what you are unable to do is essential to good parenting.

1. Think about the differences between trying to create change in our children as opposed to being humble and willing instruments of change in the hands of God. How does this shed light on the owner/ambassador discussion from the introduction?

2. Being tools of change in the hands of God is often hard, exhausting, and discouraging work. In what ways is it worth the effort?

3. Which of the temporarily effective parental power tools—fear/threats, reward, or shame/guilt do you default to when you try to control your kids? Rather than reap the sad legacy of these methods, are you willing to give yourself to the hard process of heart change in your children?

4. Put this statement in your own words: "Good parenting lives at the intersection of a humble admission of personal powerlessness and a confident rest in the power and grace of God" (p. 69–70).

5. Will you commit to surrender everything that you will do and say to the God of change who has sent you to be his representative each morning?

Chapter 5: Identity

Principle: If you are not resting as a parent in your identity in Christ, you will look for identity in your children.

1. The situation between Sally and Jamie at the beginning of this chapter may sound extreme, but most parents fall into identity amnesia at some point in their parenting journeys. Describe a time when you looked to your children for too much of your meaning and purpose.

2. Trying to get your identity from your children is a natural thing to do. What are the effects on both the parent and the child when the parent falls into this trap?

3. Which of the five indications of identity replacement (see pages 80–83) best describes your tendencies? Think of specific examples. What is your motivation in this particular area?

4. Which of the encouragements in the final paragraph of this chapter do you need to remind yourself of daily so that you are freed from asking your children to give you what they will never be able to give?

Chapter 6: Process

Principle: You must be committed as a parent to long-view parenting because change is a process and not an event.

1. Explain this quote: "Spiritual blindness happens at the intersection of deceptiveness of sin and the delusion of self-knowledge" (p. 89).

2. Have you ever gone into a time of correction with the expectation of a one-conversation turnaround? How did you feel when you had to repeat the correction at a later time? How does realizing that we are more like our children than unlike them help us deal with them in mercy and grace by not demanding instantaneous change?

3. Explain why it is important to view parenting as a life-long connected process, rather than a series of unrelated corrective encounters.

4. Have you ever considered a child's frequent need for correction to be interruptions or hassles? Would you be open, instead, to considering these moments as opportunities to be used by God in transforming the hearts and lives of your children? How would this change your attitude toward your children in these moments?

5. Identify one way your character gets in the way of parenting. How might your parenting change as you realize that you, as a parent, are being progressively transformed by God's grace, so that you will have what you need as part of his process of grace in the lives of your children?

Chapter 7: Lost

Principle: As a parent you're not dealing just with bad behavior, but a condition that causes bad behavior.

1. Have you been content to settle for surface victories and surface solutions, parenting methods that merely alleviate the symptoms but don't get to the root condition? How will understanding the focus of

the three parables in Luke 15 help you to parent with a bigger sense of purpose and direction?

2. Explain the statement, "Parenting is a moment-by-moment, day-by-day rescue mission" (p. 104). Do you find yourself resenting moments when rescue is necessary? How can you remind yourself that it is God's high calling for us to rescue our children again and again?

3. In what ways do you need to be more like the father in the parable of the lost son as you seek to rescue your lost children?

4. Which idea in the list of things that lost children need (see pages 108–9) is most eye-opening to you in your current parenting situation? Why?

5. All of our efforts to address heart issues in our children must be steeped in prayer. Will you commit to praying daily that God will open your eyes to every opportunity to address your children's heart issues, that he will empower your work as a parent, and that he will work the heart change in your children that only he can accomplish?

Chapter 8: Authority

Principle: One of the foundational heart issues in the life of every child is authority. Teaching and modeling the protective beauty of authority is one of the foundations of good parenting.

1. What makes submission to authority the central heart issue?

2. What is your responsibility as God's ambassador in matters of authority? If you are the look of God's face, the touch of his hand, and the tone of his voice, what does God's authority look like to your children?

3. Why is it crucial to follow discipline with a brief time of instruction? What keeps you from doing this on a consistent basis and how can you improve?

4. Is it a new idea for you to consider the little moments of resistance to your authority as God's grace rather than as hassles and interruptions? How can reminding yourself of his transforming grace help you to be thankful during those times?

5. What attitudes or actions concerning your use of authority do you need to confess in order to joyfully and consistently give grace to your children and point them to the hope of the cross?

Chapter 9: Foolishness

Principle: The foolishness inside your children is more dangerous to them than the temptation outside of them. Only God's grace has the power to rescue fools.

1. It is common for Christian parents to think that their job is to control their children's behavior. But I have reminded us again and again that children's behavior problems are heart problems, and that we parents are the tools God uses to work change in the hearts of our children. What steps have you recently begun to take during times of correction to get at issues of the heart with your children?

2. When your child's misbehavior gives you a picture of what controls his heart, are you willing to invest the time it takes to see this as an opportunity for heart instruction? Why is this more beneficial than the quick-fix of simply trying to control his behavior?

3. "It's . . . the propensity of our children to make their happiness the most important thing in the universe" (p. 131). They prefer to set themselves up as gods and resist your authority. How can you begin to use the key words *glory*, *wisdom*, *story*, and *welcome* in an age-appropriate ways to parent the heart of your child?

4. Have you found ways to instill in your child an awe of the glory of God as mentioned in chapter 1? If not, use one of the examples given

in the glory section of this chapter to begin naturally talking about God to your children.

5. Have you ever turned moments of ministry into moments of anger or personalized what is not personal? Take time today to confess and recognize your daily need for God's rescue and forgiveness.

Chapter 10: Character
Principle: Not all of the wrong your children do is a direct rebellion to authority; much of the wrong is the result of a lack of character.

1. Think of a time when your kids weren't doing what they should have been doing. Could their actions be the result of a lack of character, rather than direct disobedience? How did you handle the situation?

2. How does proper handling of these kinds of situations always begin? When was the last time you confessed before dealing with a character struggle?

3. In summary, "If you deal with a lack of character with a lack of character, you will not accomplish what God has given you to accomplish in the hearts of your children" (p. 139). List some steps you can begin to take to be able to see these frustrating moments not as anger-producing irritants but as moments of God-given grace.

4. Romans 1 connects character issues to worship of whatever rules the heart of your child. As you study the hearts and actions of your children, can you identify the thing(s) they have become enslaved to (e.g., control, the desire to be right or accepted, material possessions, independence, etc.)?

5. Do you need to plan a conversation with your child about heart and worship connections? Pray for God to reveal to you what your children don't understand so you can graciously show them and allow God's Spirit to do his work in their hearts.

Chapter 11: False Gods

Principle: You are parenting a worshiper, so it's important to remember that what rules your child's heart will control his behavior.

1. Explain the assertion, "Every day of our lives is a war of worship" (p. 156).

2. Identify ways you may be prone to separate Christianity from everyday life, controlling behaviors rather than focusing on what rules the heart.

3. The most important question parents can ask themselves is, "What right now does God want my child to see . . . and how can I help him see it?" (p.159).

4. Think about ways you have been tempted to confess for your children with words like, "This is what you did! And this is why you did it!" What words could you use instead to help them to examine their choices and lead them to confession?

5. Once again, this chapter ends with the need to realize and confess that we as parents also have worship struggles. List ways in which you could begin to be less judgmental and more compassionate.

Chapter 12: Control

Principle: The goal of parenting is not control of behavior but rather heart and life change.

1. How are all of the good and needed things you work to provide for your children not enough? In what ways have you become distracted and sidetracked or satisfied with a job partially done?

2. Do you ever find your child being blinded by his or her sin? Explain why it is not negative and condemning to lovingly and humbly talk to your children about their sin.

3. What is insufficient about making your children's sin just about you? When your child sins, who is in the center of his or her world? What is your child refusing to acknowledge about God when he or she chooses to sin? Think about ways you can explain this to your child in an age-appropriate way.

4. What is the difference between a child confessing that they sometimes do what is wrong and confessing that wrong lives inside them?

5. The doorway to hope is hopelessness. Explain why helping your children to understand their hopelessness is not a process of condemnation but of rescue.

Chapter 13: Rest

Principle: It is only rest in God's presence and grace that will make you a joyful and patient parent.

1. Do you ever tend to be God-forgetful, spending your mental and spiritual time meditating on the struggle and not meditating on the Lord? Commit now to memorizing Matthew 28:18–20, and in doing so, remember the one who sent you and learn to rest in him.

2. As we near the end of this book, what would you say is the ultimate job of a parent? How has your answer changed since you began studying this book?

3. What deeper goal, beyond teaching your children what to do and what not to do, are you called to as a parent? Is this an impossible task? Where is your hope as a parent found?

4. "God will expose your weaknesses so that you will run to him . . ." (p. 192). Why is this something to rejoice in rather than fear?

5. Describe how your heart can rest, knowing that God simply calls you to be faithful and not to do what only he can do.

Chapter 14: Mercy

Principle: No parent gives mercy better than one who is convinced that he desperately needs it himself.

1. What is mercy? What is mercy not? As you seek to be God's ambassador to your children, representing his character to them, take a moment to remember and list the daily mercies you receive from the Father's hands.

2. In what ways is God working on you through your children so that he can work through you for your children? Stated another way, what sin of yours are you being confronted with, exposing your own need for mercy?

3. In talking with your children about a particular behavior, what age-appropriate questions can you ask them to help them grow in heart awareness?

4. Why is it good for children to hear you confess when you've blown it?

5. Do you pray without ceasing for your children? What does prayer require you to recognize? Will you commit to covering every moment of your child's day in prayer for God's grace for them and for you?

General Index

self-control, 95
self-righteousness, 38–39, 206
self-sufficiency, 107–8
shame, 44, 67–70, 188, 192, 197–98,
    200
sin
    confessing of, 16, 69, 121, 157,
        159–60, 176, 205
    exposing of, 51, 79, 118, 122, 124,
        172–73, 177, 201
    foolishness of, 132
    presence of, 41, 52–53, 87, 113–14
    protection from, 103, 129

and spiritual blindness, 88–90, 159
    struggle with, 83, 141–42, 174–75
spiritual warfare, 17

threats, 63–65, 127

wisdom, 50, 91, 102, 109, 125–26,
    133–34, 190, 205
working parents, 26–27
worldview, 75, 91
worship, 141–43, 147–62

yelling, 42–43, 139, 200

Scripture Index

Also Available from
Paul David Tripp

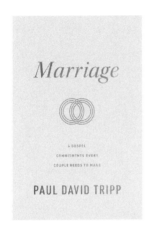

For more information, visit
crossway.org or **paultripp.com**.